T0271250

Managing Your Brand

CHANDOS

INFORMATION PROFESSIONAL SERIES

Series Editor: Ruth Rikowski
(email: Rikowskigr@aol.com)

Chandos' new series of books is aimed at the busy information professional. They have been specially commissioned to provide the reader with an authoritative view of current thinking. They are designed to provide easy-to-read and (most importantly) practical coverage of topics that are of interest to librarians and other information professionals. If you would like a full listing of current and forthcoming titles, please visit www.chandospublishing.com.

New authors: we are always pleased to receive ideas for new titles; if you would like to write a book for Chandos, please contact Dr Glyn Jones on g.jones.2@elsevier.com or telephone +44 (0) 1865 843000.C0070.

Managing Your Brand

Career Management and Personal PR
for Librarians

Julie M. Still

AMSTERDAM • BOSTON • CAMBRIDGE • HEIDELBERG
LONDON • NEW YORK • OXFORD • PARIS • SAN DIEGO
SAN FRANCISCO • SINGAPORE • SYDNEY • TOKYO
Chandos Publishing is an imprint of Elsevier

CP

CHANDOS
PUBLISHING

Chandos Publishing is an imprint of Elsevier
225 Wyman Street, Waltham, MA 02451, USA
Langford Lane, Kidlington, OX5 1GB, UK

ISBN 978-1-84334-769-9

British Library Cataloguing-in-Publication Data
A catalogue record for this book is available from the British Library

Library of Congress Control Number: 2015934371

For information on all Chandos Publishing
visit our website at http://store.elsevier.com/

Working together
to grow libraries in
developing countries

www.elsevier.com • www.bookaid.org

Contents

About the author

Julie Still is a member of the library faculty at the Paul Robeson Library, Camden Campus at Rutgers University. With a BA and MA in history and an MLS, she has worked in a variety of academic library settings, large and small, public and private. She has been active in library and campus governance and in union matters, as well as professional organizations at the state and national level. Julie has published five books, over twenty published articles, and has presented at local, state, regional, national, and international conferences. In the wider community, Julie has been active in a local trails group, the citizens' advisory committee of a bi-state transportation organization, and served as the assistant campaign treasurer for a congressional primary race.

Acknowledgements

It is impossible to write a book in a vacuum. Writing such a large manuscript affects everyone around the author. I would like to thank my colleagues at the Paul Robeson Library, especially my fellow reference librarians, Theo, John, Vib, Donna, Katie, Zara, and Laura for their patience with me when I was distracted by the book, and our director, Dr. Gary Golden, for creating such a supportive workplace. My family, Frank, Hunter, and Grace let me take over the dining room table to spread out papers, and put up with more takeout meals than usual. I was diagnosed with a chronic illness in the middle of writing the book, which caused considerable delays. Harriet and other fine people at Chandos Publishing have been very gracious about the delay in receiving the final manuscript.

Getting started

1

The phrase "managing your brand" has become a buzzword, or perhaps past the buzz-word stage. What does that actually mean? At a time when a sense of loyalty between employer and employee is passé, when it is an "everyone for themselves" world and people switch jobs frequently, it means to manage one's career, but more specifically to learn the skills needed to get a new job or enhance the current one. It also recalls an older, somewhat dated concept, that of guarding one's reputation. While this seems a little old-fashioned it is worth remembering that there are few ways of measuring a person's value in the work setting. One is money—for those in sales or product design the amount of money that any one individual or group can bring in is a sign of value.

Those in the public sector, though, can seldom point to a product or financial boost for which they can take credit. In the education field, it is even more difficult. How does one measure the value of work in education? In the K-12 arena standardized tests and other evaluative measures are currently in vogue, though certainly contro-versial. How does one define a successful teacher? In higher education departments it can be measured by how many students they graduate, how many publications and grants their faculty have, and what happens to their students after graduation—do they find jobs in their field with family sustaining wages? Libraries are even more difficult. Libraries do not graduate students and older measures, such as how many books a library houses are not as relevant in an increasingly digital age. Libraries have little or no control over whether or not students are required to use their resources to complete coursework. Librarians as individuals parse the question down further. What makes a successful librarian? Those two words are seldom used together. This may be why librarians as a group as so interested in their image. Karen G. Schneider wrote an interesting article in *American Libraries* tracking what personal branding means for librarians and provides a brief history of the term as used in librarianship. She points out that not everyone is comfortable with a high-profile image (Schneider, 2012). In a profession with a larger percentage of introverts, the idea of loud colorful self-promotion can be viewed with skepticism, if not distaste.

However, everyone has a reputation, a brand, over which they have almost sole and absolute control. This is made up of skills, work habits, intelligence and creativity, and also the ability to work well with others, to be a supportive and integral part of an organization, someone others want to be or to be around.

A track record of successful accomplishments is certainly part of that. At a tenure-track institution or an institution that offers the possibility of promotion but not tenure, being considered a likely candidate, navigating that pathway, being tenured or promoted, and then completing the circle by providing structure and support to new colleagues in the system, is a part of the academic life cycle. But the first part, nav-igating that pathway can be stressful, even at institutions with adequate support and mentoring. In some ways it is like a gothic novel:

"It was a dark and stormy night …" a clichéd beginning if ever there was one. And yet there are dark and stormy nights, metaphorical if not literal. On this dark and stormy night let us imagine a librarian, one whose tenure or promotion packet is due the next week or perhaps the next day, staring at the promotion form on the screen and asking herself, "What have I done the past five years?" Miller et al. plays upon this scenario by starting their article on tenure and promotion for serials librarians:

> *The deadline for this article is shortly before Halloween, a day associated with ghosts, witches, and scary supernatural effects. To the academic librarian, however, a much more frightening experience can be surviving the reappointment, tenure, and/ or promotion process.*
>
> Miller, McDonald, and Jia (2005, p. 40)

1.1   Why people will want to read this book

The dark and stormy night described above would truly be a nightmare, worthy of the most-talented horror film director. The tenure or promotion process is nerve-wracking enough at the best of times, with effective mentoring and a firm grasp on the process, but in the absence of either it would be gruesome indeed.

Librarians who are not eligible for tenure or academics who are not librarians still facing similar questions. How to prepare an annual report? How to plan out a career? How to include a family or outside interests? How to avoid common pitfalls? Hopefully more experienced friends and colleagues can answer some of these questions, but perhaps not as fully or as straightforward as one might like. It is also a good idea to consult more than one source, so one might talk with a mentor at one's own institution, colleagues at other institutions, and perhaps some published material as well. Advice literature abounds in many areas of life and frequently presents more pragmatic views than the friendly co-worker in the office next door. This book will hopefully do just that, provide a wider view and act as a more objective voice than on-site colleagues. To simplify matters, the language here will focus on tenure, but is equally valuable to those who are eligible for promotion without the possibility of tenure, for those who are eligible for continuing contracts (multi-year contracts that are or can be renewed on a regular basis), or those who are simply interested in career planning, including those who might intend to change careers at some point.

Career planning, especially the tenure process, is something that can be managed to a certain degree. There are always external factors coming into play. However, being prepared can remove a great deal of stress. While fortune may, indeed, favor the brave, it also favors the prepared. Many of the steps and strategies that will smooth the path of the newly hired librarian are not easily articulated by others in the profession. Memories dim, especially once one has "passed through the veil" of tenure, and not everyone can put into words the actual things they did that were helpful. Thus, while this book is aimed at the new librarian it will also be useful to those who mentor new librarians, but may have forgotten the anxiety of being a "newbie" and also the ways to alleviate that anxiety.

Having a definitive goal, like getting tenure becomes, as it should, a be all and end all. The problem with that is that once someone has reached that goal there is the inevitable "What do I do now?" There is a "post-tenure slump" that many people feel, and then set about trying to figure out what to do between that point and retirement. There may be a promotion level beyond tenure, similar to the full professor rank. In essence, after taking a year or so to recover from working towards tenure, they start over working towards the next level. Not all individuals want to do that and not all institutions offer that option. Some people might look for new challenges, ways to stretch mental and professional muscles, or reinvent themselves in some way. Some move to another position. Some decide they might wish to go into a new career or have thought about it over the years, but were not sure how to start such a transition or how to set it in motion. They remain in a job that they are no longer passionate about or even satisfied with it and spend years wishing they were elsewhere. There are times when changing jobs is not an option because of other responsibilities. In these cases, a career management plan that includes the nurturance of hobbies and outside interests can add satisfaction and texture to a life that is otherwise duty bound. Being able to reconstruct and adapt a career plan can be very helpful in deciding what future goals to set or how to adjust to circumstances beyond one's control.

In the past years, librarianship was viewed as more of a safe occupation than others, once someone had a librarian job they were likely to be able to keep it as long as they wanted, unless it was a tenurable position in which case it was more uncertain, at least in the short run. However, things can change. Economic unrest has led to the layoffs of school and public librarians. Some colleges have closed, leaving librarians unemployed. Even tenure does not bring infinite certainty. The commonly held belief that tenure provides lifelong job security is incorrect; it guarantees due process. The fine print of contracts and policy usually include some exceptions. In the case of fiscal malfeasance or a vaguer morals clause, a tenured person can be fired. Some institutions have a process for de-tenuring. More broadly, if an entire department closes the faculty in that department can often be laid off. Librarians tend to be somewhat immune from this scenario, after all, who closes the library? A few years ago, the institution where I worked faced a situation where there was serious consideration of removing the campus from the control of one university and making it a part of another. It was an unexpected possibility and, fortunately, did not come to pass. But these events do make clear that no one can ever consider their job truly "safe." There are always events arising that can negatively impact a library or department. At that point, a more experienced librarian is in the job market competing with younger applicants who are likely to have more current technological skills and a willingness to work for lower wages. It is always a good idea to be prepared for the worst, to keep a resume updated, and be able to prove one's effectiveness.

This book is intended to spell out in detail some practical things that every librarian or academician can do to avoid some common pitfalls and to adopt positive habits and practices early on to get onto the right footing. These are presented in a straightforward fashion. In some places there will be a suggested wording, a guide to things to say or write. This is not to imply that readers cannot form their own sentences, but intended as social helps, much as learning the phrases "I'm so sorry for your loss" and "I'm sure they will be very happy together" can smooth the way at funerals and weddings, regardless of one's real feelings about the dearly departed or newly married.

While cynicism is in vogue and the clever sound bite is considered more valuable than a friendly word of encouragement, this book is written with a realistic but hopeful frame of mind. It is detailed and thorough but not hard driving. I prefer to watch TED Talks (technology, education, design) and read studies of what makes people happy than books on how to get ahead by besting the next guy.

Most of all, I hope that readers will find this book somewhat comforting and that it will alleviate some fears and anxieties, that some of the suggestions herein will prove useful. Not everyone will find everything applicable to their own situation, but hopefully everyone will find something.

1.2 Structure of the book

The book is arranged for the newly hired or the job seeker. The seasoned librarian may want to skip directly to specific chapters depending on their most pressing concern at the moment. The book starts with setting out a career plan, deciding on some goals, and how to achieve them. The goal may be as simple as "find a job," or it may be as complicated as "plan a career that will put me in a position to be the director of an ARL library." As disparate as those may seem there are common threads to both. The chapter discusses how to decide on a career goal and then how to decide where one is in relation to that goal, and how to create a map to reach it. The hardest part is deciding on a goal, really understanding what it is one wants. Sometimes, it is not as apparent as it seems. The chapter walks through a couple of scenarios, winnowing down or widening out the particular goals. The section on "understanding where you are" goes into detail on learning what is expected of a tenure-track librarian, and the importance of reading contract and policy documents.

The second chapter deals with basic record keeping and general strategies. It is sad but true that many an empire has been lost due to poor-record keeping and communication (even if that communication is only with oneself). It is this chapter, more so than any other, that can make the difference between achieving a goal and not, because no matter how effective one is at all of the other areas discussed in the book, if it is not documented it does not matter. Some things, of course, cannot be measured in their entirety, but almost everything can be recorded in some fashion and be used in promotional materials.

The next three chapters concern the three basic components of a tenure packet, librarianship (or teaching), scholarship (presenting and publishing), and service (active on the institution level or in professional associations). These are the three legs of the stool for all the areas of academic life, and every tenure contender needs to show some level of success in all the three. The mix will depend on the individual institution and the strengths and weaknesses of the individual person, as well as the opportunities available. The three are interconnected and often build upon each other.

The seventh chapter takes the strategies developed in the first two chapters and applied in the next three chapters, and then extends them further. The crux of this chapter is using the basic foundations set up in the first and second chapter, and then applying them to librarianship, scholarship, and research. It is taking things apart into small pieces and then building something else with them; it is stretching outward or upward or around, going from where you are to where you want to be. This last chapter is on putting it all together.

Each chapter is broken down into sections. Where possible, or feasible, very concrete suggestions are given, down to the most basic level, including how to monitor one's progress. As previously mentioned, there will be suggestions on things to say or to write.

Some suggestions for further reading will be provided, as will standard bibliographic endnotes, for those who wish to investigate further or find the source materials used.

1.3 Author credentials

Those who know me in person might be quick to point out that I have not followed all of the advice presented in this book. They would be correct. Not every suggestion in this book will be suitable for all readers, and it is written for an audience of more than one. Different people will have different ways of doing things and I intend to offer suggestions gleaned from wider experience than simply my own. Other sources consulted are listed in the bibliography. And there are always those times when we can see so clearly what we ought to do, but cannot quite bring ourselves to do it. It is also true that the best teacher is not necessarily someone who learned their subject matter quickly or easily or seemed to know it innately, but someone who had to struggle to learn it. Many of the items in this book are things I learned only through trial and error. Some are the results of mistakes I made and could not repair. Some are goals that I have never been able to meet (and likely never will). Some are suggestions that others have made in person or in print that I wish I had known earlier or that would not work for me, but will certainly be of benefit to others.

The basics are simple, I have a masters of arts in library science (University of Missouri), a masters of arts in history (University of Richmond), employed at a number of institutions in the early part of my career, some large, some small, some private, some public, some pastoral, and some urban. Some had continuing contracts and others did not. I have known the agony of defeat, being told my contract would not be renewed, and the thrill of victory, tenure at Rutgers University Libraries and a long and happy career there. This is my sixth book and as of this writing I have published nearly 40 articles, proceedings, and book chapters, some peer reviewed, some not. I have given talks at conferences, small, local, regional, state, national, and international. Earlier in my career, I was very active in professional associations, but as family responsibilities became more pressing this has shifted to institutional service, and activities were based more on place than wider opportunity.

While many librarians focus all of their interests and energies on our shared profession, one of my career themes has been taking librarianship out of the building and into other areas. I have also always had outside interests, which are not necessarily ones commonly found among librarians, and many of the points presented here were learned in those other venues. Among those interests are business and politics, which converge in community work. While I have been a librarian for nearly 30 years, and have enjoyed it, the variety of libraries I have worked at have given me an appreciation for how large institutions, small institutions, small parts of larger institutions, public universities, private colleges, libraries that offer tenure, faculty status but not tenure, multi-year contracts but not tenure, unionized librarians, non-union libraries, and any number of combinations, are different and similar. Being married to a librarian who has worked at other institutions has given me some understanding of how those institutions work as well.

I have also enjoyed being involved in other kinds of activities. One of these, as mentioned, is business. I read business publications; *Working Woman* magazine was a tremendous help to me and I have mourned its end in 2002; the *Wall Street Journal* is another. There is a great deal to be learned from business publications, including advice books. Advice for women in business frequently transfers to women in academia, though often with some adaptations. It is also very useful to see the world through another lens. Being involved in an extended family investment club also provided me with some useful skills in evaluating corporate behavior. Politics is another interest. Librarians were early adaptors to web technology and I became the web manager of my state representative's campaign website. Later when she decided to run for Congress I was the assistant campaign treasurer, which means I filed the Federal Election Commission (FEC) campaign finance reports, but resigned when that came to require more time than I could provide. If those FEC reports are not filed correctly someone can go to jail; it proved too stressful to combine making sure they were accurate with the demands of a full-time day job and two young children. Since then my political involvement has been more of the armchair variety. However, the business and politics interests converged when I was invited to the President's Economic Forum in 2002. I was the only librarian in attendance and my skills turned out to be very valuable.

Administrative responsibilities are often viewed solely through the director's office, but there are a number of other pathways to these duties. Having an interest in politics and public policy is a very effective training ground. Early in my career I thought I might want to be a library director, but some research in that area showed me that it was not a good fit for my skills and personality. However, I have enjoyed being the president of the campus faculty union and representing the library on other administrative bodies. None of these were positions that required much effort to get—no one else wanted them. To each of their own. It is something I like doing and feel I have some talent for (sitting in a chair eating free food being a strength of mine).

A third interest, this one shared by many, is family. I had two children while on tenure track and had to learn how to balance work and parenting responsibilities. Helpful colleagues played a major role in that effort, as did an involved spouse. I am or have been a PTA officer, an elementary school room mother, a Scout leader, and a service activity coordinator. All of these roles have helped me learn new skills, and have also provided me with another area to use my skills as a librarian. Like all parents who work outside the home there has been a great deal of juggling. There was the day I dressed carefully because I was driving to a statewide convention to receive an award and the baby threw up on my shoulder. The day I had to ask a colleague to give a class presentation in my stead because one of the kids was sick and my husband was away. The evenings and weekends that used to be partially devoted to reading and writing were now taken up with being a study partner for spelling tests, reading over paper drafts, filling out endless school forms, and listening to long treatises on the current state of playground drama.

While not everyone has children, few people get through life without some family connections. Parents, as they get older, require more care. I do recall a frantic day when I needed to leave on time to pick up a child before the daycare closed, the other woman working in the library needed to leave on time because her 90-year-old mother's care giver's shift was ending, and the person due to relieve her was late. We stared at each other trying to figure out what to do. Family responsibilities of one sort or another impact most employees at some point. This factor will be taken into account throughout the book.

Taken all together it represents a life lived fully, both at work and at home. It has been my pleasure to note not only the strategies I have learned and used, but to talk with colleagues near and far about strategies they themselves have learned and used. Some work, some do not, sometimes opportunities pass one by, sometimes they come around again, and sometimes they do not.

I hope that readers will find this book of use, even if only to affirm their own decisions or beliefs. Surely each reader will find one or two new ideas or strategies that might be helpful. Having had the good fortune to be mentored by talented and caring people, and having mentored, in one way or another, a number of librarians, there are certain truths or commonalities that become clear. This book is intended to share those solutions, the ones developed and the ones found in secondary sources or by talking with colleagues, with the profession at large.

Planning your pathway

2

There is a simplicity to entering into a new venture. One walks through the doors of a new workplace and begins a journey, goes on an adventure, and enters a pre-existing culture, a unique human ecosystem with written and unwritten rules. Brand new possibilities await and all sorts of things could happen. Being open to opportunities is essential, but it is also essential to have some idea about what sort of opportunities will bring the most satisfaction. In a tenure situation getting tenure may be the immediate goal, or it might be simply keeping the job or working towards a next career stop. This chapter will go over some ways of being prepared and ready.

2.1 Deciding what you want

Deciding on a goal is often the hardest part of a career or personal pathway. Take for instance the often mentioned "I'd like to write." On the face of it, this is simple. What is required? Anyone with an access to a computer can write. No computer? Surely paper and pen are available. No? There is always chalk and sidewalks or a finger in the sand. People have been writing using these and equally exalted and humble methods for millennia. Someone who says "I'd like to write" and is not actually writing probably means something else entirely.

More frequently an expression wished to write is actually a desire to be read, but this also is not as simple as it seems. After all, graffiti artists in busy train stations are read. So are STOP signs, the back of cereal boxes, and tax forms. Yet people who say they wish to write (and really mean they want to be read) would not be content with that.

Perhaps the goal is to be published. Who would not enjoy seeing their name in print as an author or writer? Blogs and self-publishing have broken down some of these walls. Anyone can start up an online column or contribute to existing ones. Authors willing to expend their own money can self-publish a book. There may not be as many publishing houses as there used to be, but there are still quite a few out there. Someone who says they want to write (and means they want to be published), but has not submitted anything to a publisher or publication does not really mean that what they want is to write.

Some people who say they want to write may mean they wish they could make their living writing. There is a hazy vision of spending days at the keyboard or typewriter or paper notebook, mailing off articles or manuscripts and collecting royalty checks and fan letters from the mailbox. People who make their living writing, however, view it as a business. They write primarily when they are paid to do so. Mortgage, groceries, and orthodontia are dependent upon writing something that will sell, not necessarily what they would like to be writing. Full-time writers (novelists, independent scholars, and the like) are self-employed and have the same problems that small business owners do; they struggle with health insurance (unless a spouse provides it) and do not get paid if they are not working every day. There is no paid sick time, no paid vacation, and no professional development money.

This is a far cry from saying "I'd like to write." People who want to write will write. What they need to find is a way of making their writing useful to other aspects of their life, or a way to earn enough from their pen to pay the bills. That may mean they often write what is saleable not necessarily what they most wish to express. Someone who says they want to write, or want to write for living do not always envision that as writing computer manuals or non-fiction pieces on investment options or grant applications. People who want to write might find a job that involves writing as a part of their work, but it is not the main part, or what they write is academic or professional in nature. It is not in the same ballpark as being a renowned literary novelist, but it is being paid to write. The important thing is to discover what is actually meant by "I want to write."

Being a small business owner (other than self-employed writer) is another common dream. In *Millionaire Woman Next Door*, author Thomas Stanley found that many small businesses fail because the owner wanted to be an entrepreneur, but did not do the right kind of research. Women who started gift shops often did so because they liked gifts or receiving gifts, not because that was a profitable industry (Stanley, 206). Those women would have been better off going into other types of businesses, after doing the research on what was profitable in their geographic area, or what businesses were needed. In more recent years those who are interested in businesses that are not profitable in brick and mortar format might try online ventures, such as etsy.com, but assuming it is possible to make a living from such work is, perhaps, not wise. Starting a self-service laundry might be more profitable.

Sometimes goals are simple: *I want to get a job*, or, *I want to keep my job or maintain a level of standing in my occupation that it will be easier to find a job if I lose this one*. That is a worthy goal in any economy and any occupation, especially if others are dependent upon you for daily necessities. Certainly new graduates are advised to take a first job that may not exactly match their talents or interests, as a springboard to a second job that will be a better fit. Someone who has lost a job will probably have the simple goal of finding another one. Librarians at tenure-track institutions will likely have a goal of receiving tenure. However, in Maslow's basic hierarchy of needs, if the basic survival needs are met, people look for self-actualization. They want not just any job, but a job they would enjoy that provides some sense of worth in addition to a paycheck. For others, earning as much money as possible is the goal, or a step to a goal such as early retirement. So it is not just getting a job, but thinking about what kind of job and why, or whether having a job that met basic needs could be supplemented by other forms of activity, family, or hobbies, that created a sense of self. Some things are better left as hobbies. Someone with a love of painting might go into another field and save their artistic endeavors as a way to relax, something they do only to please themselves.

Other goals are more complex or specific, such as *I want to be the director of an ARL library* or *I want to work at a small liberal arts college* or *I want to have a job that values my writing ability*. Some are a little muddier: *I want to have a job in an area that will let me go boating frequently* or *I want a job that will let me be near my elderly parents.* When someone says they want to be a library director or a department head it is always interesting to ask what they like about those jobs. If the answer is "I like to be in charge," that person is in trouble. Library directors seldom view themselves as being in charge. They are usually the only person with that title on their campus. It can be lonely. At small institutions with limited administrative staff, the library director spends a lot of time dealing with things like elevator problems and complaints about the temperature in the building or late fees. At large institutions, the library director must devote considerable time to fundraising. At all institutions, library directors answer to provosts, chancellors, or chief information officers who may have little knowledge of or interest in libraries. They must manage a staff of imperfect people all equipped with egos and quirks. This will all be very frustrating to someone who went into the job to "be in charge." Someone who approaches directorship with the willingness to learn about elevators and HVAC systems in order to earn a higher salary might be happier, having more realistic expectations.

The helping professions, such as teaching, librarianship, and nursing, generally involve coming into contact with others. Arlie Hochchild's excellent book *The Managed Heart* discusses the often contrasting expectations of people. Her book compared the behaviors expected of repossession firm employees with those of flight attendants, and the gender biases inherent therein. Librarians, while not flight attendants, also sometimes encounter expectations. People often are unsure of exactly what questions they want answered or how they want the information they are seeking, but they do generally expect courteous treatment, and can confuse professional helpful service with friendship.

Someone who is more introverted or prefers to keep human contact to a minimum should take this into account when deciding what type of job to aim for. Those who do not enjoy the company of small children should shy away from pediatric nursing, elementary schools, or school libraries.

Asking people who are already in a job what the job is like or what their career path has been like can be a fruitful endeavor, providing useful information, but advice often differs depending on whom one is asking. This is especially true in matters pertaining to work/family balance. Some advise those who know they wish to have children or know they will have other family responsibilities to plan out their career with that in mind. Others, such as Sheryl Sandberg in her book *Lean In*, say not to do that, not to avoid opportunities that do not fit one's end game. She writes:

> *What I am arguing is that the time to scale back is when a break is needed or when a child arrives—not before, and certainly not years in advance. The months and years leading up to having children are not the time to lean back, but the critical time to lean in.*
>
> Sandberg, 95

Decisions on family matters are personal and must be made at the individual level. Those who have or will soon be deciding whether or not to have children should ask how family friendly a workplace is. One would not want to make a big move, pulling a spouse along, to a job without a lot of other opportunities around, and a year later need to move again for family reasons, at least not without knowing that in advance so financial preparations can be made. These can be tricky questions to ask in a job interview, but looking for cues in the way people at that institution talk can provide some idea of whether or not the people there have family responsibilities and how open they are talking about them. When we are interviewing I try to make a point of mentioning that our workplace is family friendly, as evidenced by the fact that most of the librarians have children who are, or were, young when we were on tenure track.

A 2008 study by Graves, Xiong, and Park found that librarians had fewer children than faculty in other disciplines, which they theorize is because librarianship is a predominantly female field and women tend to feel that the demands of family and children negatively impact their ability to meet tenure and promotion requirements more so than men. However, male librarians also feel the time constraints of having young children while on tenure track. Todd Spires writes about his children in his 2007 article on tenure for librarians. James Lang, in his 2005 memoir of life as a first year academic, also writes about balancing the demands of teaching and scholarship with having young children. Libraries that want to attract younger librarians, of either gender, need to make clear what accommodations the institution makes for people who have family responsibilities. It should not be seen as exceptions to the rule, but as part of the rule.

Generally, though, job seekers simply want to find a job that suits them, their talents and abilities. College career centers have tests available to help students and alumni discover their personality types and what kind of jobs best suit those traits. There is a number of self-help/discovery books that provide guidance on finding out the best job fit for individual readers. *What Color is Your Parachute* by Richard Bolles is perhaps the best known of these. It was originally self-published in 1970 and picked up by a commercial publisher a few years later and still in print today. The book is revised annually, sometimes more frequently than that.

Deciding what one wants is also important in dealing with people. Keeping one's "eyes on the prize" has the effect of minimizing daily distractions. The actions of others that might at other times appear rude or intentionally slighting fall by the wayside if the end goal is kept in mind. There is an apocryphal story from the early days of personal computers about a businesswoman who needed an office computer repaired. She went to her company's computer person for advice. He looked at her and said "I don't like you." She said, "That's okay. I need your advice on ..." and described the issue. He answered her and she was able to fix the computer problem. She would have had every right to object to his attitude, but she needed her computer fixed. There would be time for complaints later. This is not to say that the issues at hand in that situation were not serious or did not to be addressed, but the woman's primary focus at that moment was getting her computer fixed and she stayed focused on that, kicking up a fuss about interpersonal behaviors is only productive if there is some end game in mind. Changing a hostile or destructive atmosphere is most definitely a worthy goal; it just may not be the most immediate goal.

Having the end goal in mind helps arrange a daily or weekly work schedule. Achieving tenure means, having time set aside for research and/or service in professional organizations. That requires some control over one's work day. If a particular task or interaction disrupts a chain of thought on a regular basis throughout the day perhaps those interruptions can be bundled so several are dealt with at one point during the day or at a specific time during the week. Having a goal also helps with long-range planning. In *Women of Academe*, Nadya Aisenberg and Mona Harrington point out that "perhaps the most important specific rule is to plan strategically for a career, to make five-year plans and ten-year plans as part of a process of conscious decision making" (Aisenberg & Harrington, 1988, p. 146). They point out that "what is crucial is the middle-range planning, the projections of ends and means for several years ahead" (Aisenberg & Harrington, 1988, p. 146). Todd Spires, writing in *Illinois Libraries*, suggest putting timelines into planning—not just to write an article, but to complete an article by a specific date. For him, this takes an abstract idea and makes it more concrete. He also hangs a copy of his goals in a place where he will see it every day.

It is important to recognize that goals change over time. What anyone wants in their 20's is likely to be much different from what they want in their 50's. Periodic revisiting of goals is a must. As mentioned in other chapters, if a librarian focuses on getting tenure, there can be an emotional slump afterward. The goal has been met—What is next? The goal of running for office in a national professional association may fade once the prospective candidate realizes how much time and energy the position would take, and how much travel it would include.

Whatever aids or guidance one chooses, it is impossible, or at least unadvisable, to go forward without knowing what it is one wants. Once that is decided, at least generally, it is time for the next step.

2.2 Developing a personal mission statement

Deciding on goals is easier with a personal mission statement. It is important to have some concept of prioritization in one's efforts. Granted, priorities shift over time, sometimes over the course of a day, but long-term and short-term goals tend to stay in place. Personal mission statements should not be overly specific or address self-created time lines. Five-year plans can be effective, but there is often much about them that is more reliant on outside forces than internal drive and effort. Stephen Covey in the well-regarded *The Seven Habits of Highly Effective People* suggests a visualization technique, imaging oneself in the position or circumstances desired. In that book he recommends envisioning your own funeral, listening to what you hope people would say about you, and then working to become that person (Covey, 1989, pp. 96–99). It provides a goal, which, if focused upon, will drown out distractions. As mentioned earlier, a clear focus will make the squabbles, momentary difficulties, and daily interruptions seem unimportant, as merely part of the background scenery, passing images in the larger picture. In another of his books, *The Seven Habits of Highly Effective Families*, Covey writes a chapter on creating a family mission statement. He uses a variety of metaphors to convey the importance of deciding on principles around which to build family life. One metaphor is a construction site where everyone is busy, but no one knows exactly what they are building. Another is an airplane loading passengers and fuel, but with no clear destination in mind (Covey, 1997, pp. 72–73).

A personal mission statement is not *I want to be a library director in five years*. A personal mission statement would be more along the lines of *I want to be in a position of responsibility in the knowledge industry*. After all, if someone focuses on becoming a library director he or she might miss the opportunity to become the head of a digitization center on a dynamic college campus, or an opportunity to take a job as the assistant head of product development at a reputable content management firm. A personal mission statement might be *I would like a job that would allow me to do research that is of interest to me*. That could be done in a number of places, one certainly being at a library or an academic institution. A flexible personal mission statement, as opposed to a more specific one, also allows the option of walking away from one situation and trying another. Sometimes the desired end result is not worth the aggravation it would take to achieve it, at least in that particular setting, but a similar, equally acceptable result, can be found in a different setting.

Other factors can come into play. An ill parent or a spouse's job might keep someone in a particular geographic area. Their personal mission statement might involve developing the skills they would need to progress professionally once they are able to move. Fulfillment might not come in the job area at all. A position of responsibility in the knowledge industry might mean becoming the volunteer chair of the local historical society and setting up archival standards or digitizing their collections, and then a few years down the line, when job opportunities are better or family responsibilities lessen, parlaying that into a lateral move at one's current job or a new one somewhere else.

A less-specific personal mission statement might also show other priorities. The siren song of tuition benefits for children might lead to a job that is less personally fulfilling, but financially beneficial for a few years. Sometimes goals are a means to an end. Vice President Joe Biden went to law school, but not with the goal of being a lawyer. He wanted to go into politics and researched the biographical data of those in elected office. Most were lawyers, so he went to law school (Biden, 2007, p. 26).

At times a personal mission statement is not focused on a "what" but a "who." In other words, what sort of person does one want to be as opposed to what sort of job does one want. Behavioral shifts can be more difficult than job hunting. It is certainly harder. As an example, if a directorship or other position of authority is a goal (for financial or personal reasons), ask what qualities someone in that job has. Are they responsible, trustworthy, adept at organization, socially skilled? Read studies of people in those positions and job descriptions. Find out what those people have or are. Learn what personal traits they have that can be studied or learned. Or simply think about what needs to change to reach the intended goal. There are some things that might need to be adjusted. Someone who is five feet tall is unlikely to become a basketball player, but he could become a basketball coach or a team doctor. A music librarian may be someone who loves music, but knew that she did not want to pursue a life as a musician. A systems librarian may have considered life as an entrepreneur, but decided against it because family responsibilities required a dependable consistent income and benefits. Finding a job that allowed each of them to be involved in their passion was a personal mission statement that led them to a fulfilling career they might not have thought of at the start of their work lives.

A personal mission statement should also include at least a nod to a life outside of work. Those who are entirely consumed by their job are quicker to burnout. A personal identity defined completely and solely by work is not healthy, nor does it bode well for retirement. Beyond simple factors such as maintaining good diet and exercise habits, which reduce stress and susceptibility to illness, everyone should have at least one outside interest. It could simply be family, whether a family by blood or choice, but a connection to people who view each other as something besides an occupation. Po Bronson, author of *What Should I Do With My Life* and co-author of *Top Dog: The Science of Winning and Losing*, was asked how to avoid burnout. He said "You need periods of rest and recuperation. You can get that from your personal life" (Rosato, 2013, p. 94). Few of us will die on the job, which means there will be some part of life after retirement, whether that retirement is by choice or not. An outside hobby will keep life after work interesting. No matter how devoted someone has been to their job, it will carry on without them. As Sydney Lagier wrote in the *Wall Street Journal*:

> When I retired five years ago, the company I worked for hired a new chief financial officer to take over my green eyeshades. I kept thinking my successor would need to call me with questions that, of course, only I would know the answer to. I was there for 18 years. You couldn't possibly replace an 18-year veteran with someone new and not expect a little turmoil.
> But he never called. The company operated just fine without me.
>
> Lagier (2013, p. R12)

No one is indispensable. Regardless of how powerful or influential an individual has been, the day after they leave their job for the last time their influence is over. Someone might have developed workflows or built strong book collections or started a research center, but those routines and materials can change or end under another's direction. Percy Bysshe Shelley's poem "Ozymandias" should be required reading for all who think they will leave a lasting physical legacy.

Outside interests are also a deterrent to living in a bubble. Librarians who only socialize with librarians can easily come to assume that everyone knows the professional jargon, that everyone is computer literate, aware of funding issues, and in general well versed in library matters. Spending some time with non-librarians, whether other parents involved in a child's extracurricular activity, a health and nutrition group, religious organization, or a community group, or chatting with strangers at ballgames or theatrical productions helps maintain a healthy connection to the "real world." This can be very useful when connecting to potential donors, students or member of the public at service desks, or when meeting elected officials at public events. Knowing how to speak and interact with people who are not immersed in the same occupational stew every day is a necessity, especially when preparing a tenure packet—not everyone reading and evaluating it will have significant knowledge of libraries or librarians. Being able to explain in layman's terms what one does and how it fits into the larger picture is a necessary part of the process.

Having a non-library contact list is also instrumental in garnering community support for local public libraries or local campuses. If there is a legislative hearing and having people in the community speak upon your behalf would be helpful, or would be crucial, it is important to be able to reach out and get that support.

A personal mission statement simply clarifies one's intent. It is the channel one will sail through, or at least the channel one intends to sail through. It is the individual version of an institutional mission statement. The personal mission statement is also a form of the standard "elevator talk." Should a new librarian find themselves in an elevator with the library director or the campus chancellor or the president of your chosen ALA section and that person says "What are your plans?" it is a good idea to have an answer on hand. This would not require all of the details but an "I enjoy my job and look forward to new challenges. I'd like to develop some courses/classes in X" or "I work with some wonderful people and we want to strengthen our outreach to campus groups" or "I'm looking for opportunities to develop my leadership skills."

2.3 Understanding where you are

Once a destination, in general, has been decided upon it is a good idea to take a look around and see where one is at the moment. This would seem to be common sense, but, as will be discussed later, common sense usually is not very common at all. Before starting on a journey one should always know one's starting point. A recent college graduate who wants to be a librarian can tally up her spot as someone with an undergraduate degree. A newly hired tenure-track librarian is at the start of that process. Someone on the job market should take stock and set priorities. In the best of all worlds in what sort of library would that person wish to work, public, academic, special, or other? What size of institution? What parts of the country would he or she want to work in? Jobs fitting the most criteria would be the ones most desired.

A job candidate is in another position. At that point the search committee has already decided the candidate has the paper-based criteria for the job; the interview is to decide whether or not the candidate is someone they want to work with for the next 5 or 10 years. The in-person interview can be confusing for candidates who think the focus of the day is on them; in part it is, but just as brides think the wedding day is about them (and it is), it is also an opportunity for people to talk to each other, reminisce, have fun, and size up the new member of the family. At an interview, the candidate expects that the search committee will be familiar with her resume and cover letter, but very few candidates have done similar research on the library. Look at the website and find out about the interests and job areas of the librarians and staff there, especially of the people you will be meeting. See if contracts or other job information is made publically available. Watch the interactions among people at the interview. The relationships on paper are seldom how things actually work. Do people get along well, do they laugh with each other, do they seem to like and support each other? How does the director interact with librarians and staff? How does the library fit in to the university? If the candidate takes a tour of campus, do the librarians and staff interact with other people on campus? Is it a place where you would want to spend a few or several years?

Savvy candidates will ask questions like "What would you want the successful job candidate to have accomplished in his or her first year?" That provides an opportunity for both sides to basically put together the job, and see if it is a good fit for the candidate and the institution.

There are other, esoteric factors to consider. A librarian who ultimately wants to devote a great deal of his time to instruction and is in or takes a job that does not involve a lot of that has a variety of options. He can consider his current job a stepping stone or perhaps there is an instruction librarian on staff who will be old enough to retire in a few years. Less fortunately, there may have been another librarian hired at the same time whose job does involve a lot of instruction. There may be ways of developing classes or workshops in another area within the institution, to create an area of strength that is separate from the existing programs. Here again, outside interests can help fill a gap. There are other ways to develop or maintain instructional skills, for example, being an adjunct teacher at a local college or teaching through a community center. Someone who wants to keep cataloging skills from getting rusty while in a job that does not include that job duty might volunteer to catalog a church or synagogue library or historical society. Web and social media skills can be honed through outside interests.

As the journey progresses it is important to keep in mind where one is along the path. In other words, the traveler's position changes both in and of itself and in relationship to the end goal, which may also change over time. This is akin to checking the map along the way, which streets or towns have been passed and what is next. This is helpful in gauging how far along one should be on individual tasks and also on the goal in general. There is a tenure clock which makes it easy to see how close the candidate is getting to the deadline. Benchmarks can be very useful. Initial contracts followed by a review and if successful then one or more subsequent contracts leading up to a tenure decision offer set points along the way. Some institutions have evaluation points for every 2 years, some three, some require an annual evaluation. Each of these offers the opportunity for re-assessment and recalculation, shifting goals and priorities around as needed or recommended.

The newly hired librarian, especially in her first job, may find the adjustment from being a graduate student to being a faculty member more difficult than she might have expected. Graduate students are scrappy outsiders, and often activists; there is an "us against them" view of the faculty. Suddenly they find themselves part of the establishment, one of "them." Someone who was on the job market can find him or herself on a search committee a few months later, now one of the privileged few who inevitably must evaluate and reject qualified and personable candidates. This is a larger mental shift that one might think. New classroom faculty have to adjust to being the person who grades as opposed to the student who is graded. Frank Furstenberg, in *Behind the Academic Curtain* writes: "When you cross over from student to faculty member, it is not uncommon to revisit the feelings that many of you had on entering your doctoral program: self-doubt, confusion, uncertainty, and occasionally even dread" (Furstenberg, 2013; 74). Later on that same page he writes "Entering a new role, even one that you have prepared for much of your life, is genuinely daunting." It involves a change in self-perception. There are new expectations and rules. The unflattering stereotype of college graduate who still wants to be part of the dorm or fraternity culture when he needs to move on to another phase of his life is one to be avoided.

Even after the tenure decision, the journey continues and any one individual's position continues to change. Every new hire stops being the new hire when someone else comes on board. One librarian described this as becoming "last year's Christmas toy." The newness wears off, just as the youngest child in the family moves up to being a middle child when a new baby is born. Suddenly, the new middle child is not as cute as he or she used to be. Every senior librarian was once a new hire. A librarian accustomed to being the only man, woman, Hispanic, redhead, twenty something, or cat lover can easily lose the "only" status. Sometimes that is good, sometimes it is bad, but it is always a change, not only in how people view each other but in how people view themselves. After a successful tenure decision the librarian suddenly has more gravitas, by the stroke of a pen, that person ceases to be a mentee and suddenly moves into the mentor category. As with search committees, a librarian can be up for tenure 1 year and on the tenure committee for someone else the next. There are certain things that tenured or more senior librarians or faculty can do, that really only they can do, and they have a responsibility to do. I make a point of showing an id upon every entrance to the library, after going out of the building for a meeting, after running out for an afternoon snack, after leaving and re-entering the building for any reason. This is required of all visitors. It is all too easy for employees to think that, since the guard at the door knows them, they do not have to do this. This can cause problems for the guard who does not challenge staff but does challenge visitors to show id. This can lead to discrimination claims. If more senior employees set the example that everyone needs to show an id, it is more likely that all employees will do so. The door id is just one instance; there are many other ways that senior librarians create an institutional culture. As someone who benefited from a family friendly organizational culture that supported me through two pregnancies and parenting, I have an obligation to continue that culture for the people who were hired after me, to take their desk time or classes when they call in with sick kids or on days when there is a classroom party, as my colleagues had done for me. There are some perks with seniority, a bigger office perhaps, but flaunting the rules that others must follow is not one of them. Just as a middle aged person acting like a teenager is inappropriate so it is inappropriate for someone with seniority to maintain the attitudes of a new employee, the enthusiasm and innovation yes, but all the attitudes and viewpoints, no.

Getting feedback is essential. An annual review or at least an informal meeting is a good benchmark. If possible feedback should be in a recordable form; written is best. That provides guidelines for the next year or to work towards the end goal or the next measurable point. It also allows time for improvement. No one wants a nasty surprise at reappointment or tenure. If there are problems there should be a formal mechanism for addressing them, or at least knowing about them. Savvy directors will ask a candidate or tenure-track librarian's colleagues for feedback. If no one expresses any concerns at points along the way it is difficult for them to vote against that person at the tenure decision. Someone being evaluated might ask questions like "What do you think I should have accomplished by the next evaluation point?" and "What areas do you think I need to work on most?" and "What do you see as being the most problematic areas of my work?" and "What suggestions would you have for me?"

Informal feedback and information gathering is just as useful. Look for opportunities to ask tenured librarians, especially recently tenured librarians, what they thought counted the most, or what the process was like. Talking with a few people will hopefully bring forth a consensus on the items that would be needed in any future packet. If there have been unsuccessful tenure candidates try (delicately) to find out what happened. I once took a job which had had a lot of turnover. In part it was necessity and in part it was youthful arrogance, thinking I could easily succeed where others had failed. In a relatively short period of time I found myself in the same situation as my predecessors and started looking for another position. Institutions that have a lot of churn (turnover) in general or in a specific position should take stock. Are there inherent flaws in the job description or in the way the job is structured? Are the wrong people being hired for the job?

In a larger environment candidates should know who else is in their pack or class. How many people will be going up for tenure at the same time? This will change, of course, as some people will leave before coming up for tenure, others may go up early or drop back a year (if this is allowable). Generally speaking tenure candidates are not compared to each other but to the standard criteria. However, it is difficult for a tenure committee not to see how candidates stack up against each other. This is especially true if more than one candidate has a similar job title or description. Knowing who else is in the pack allows each candidate to develop a particular specialty or research interest that is distinctive. Keep track of who is in the class over time. In addition to people dropping out, new hires may go up early. What started as a pack of four can easily be reduced to one or two, or what started out as a group of one can become two or three.

2.4   Creating a map

Getting from point A to point B geographically is easier than it used to be, thanks to technology like gps systems. Other journeys are a bit more difficult, even when the route is known. For example, if someone wants to lose weight the two simplest strategies are to eat less and exercise more. Those are fairly simple, yet more diet books are written each year. There is a never ending line of experts telling acolytes what they should and should not do, and inventors telling buyers that their own particular trick or device will provide instant results. It seldom works. The eat less/exercise more method is the most effective; it is just not always easy to do, simple though the strategy may be. Similarly, the way to accumulate wealth is to spend less and save more. Again, this is more easily said than done, though the concept is a simple one.

One basic way to keep on task is to figure out what internal roadblocks are at work. As an example, someone who wants to go to the gym but does not, realizes it is because her gym clothes are in another room and it often seems too difficult to go get them. When she moved her gym clothes to a more convenient place she went to the gym more. When trying to save money I realized I was spending too much on lunches and wanted to brown bag more often. However, keeping track of plastic utensils was an issue—they broke, they got lost in the bag, and so on. A local charity shop offered nice silver utensils for twenty-five cents each. One dollar bought two forks and two spoons, kept in a desk drawer and washed off after each use. That simple step has made a big difference in how often lunch is brought from home. People who are easily distracted by email can set aside certain times of the day to read and respond to messages, and ignore new emails in between. When working towards a goal it is important to figure out what roadblocks we put in our own way, and what we can do to remove them. Fear of success is as debilitating as fear of failure. A lack of confidence in ourselves, a sense that we could never achieve our goals, is as much or more of a detriment than the rejection or refusal of others. The Greek oracle said "Know yourself." This is true of our weaknesses as well as our strengths. Some traits are neither but merely a part of our personalities. Some people tackle weighty issues better in the morning and routine matters in the afternoon, for others it is the reverse. Some people prefer to work alone, others prefer group projects. Knowing oneself allows for better planning, not just on day-to-day issues but also for long-term projects and -goals.

There are also external roadblocks. What institutional, technological or interpersonal factors are preventing the implementation of a personal or institutional project, and what can be done to remove or go around them? Sometimes it is as simple as finding a way to exempt the one person who objects to a particular new program, or to ask them to participate in a different way.

Sometimes it is finding a way to re-cast the project in a different light, tying it to an institutional goal or changing the words used so it sounds like something more acceptable. Changing the name of something can be a quick solution to many problems. When I was preparing the thesis for a master's degree in history, and had an initial draft completed for an initial review, one of the faculty on my committee pointed out that I had not answered the question set out in the title. I left the meeting feeling hopeless, certain that I would have to start anew. A friend who was reading the document for me, who had sat through many such meetings as part of thesis committees at another school, gently suggested that I change the title and the introduction. When I broached this with my advisor he decided that was acceptable. On a more mundane basis, many suburban naturalists have despaired over how to keep squirrels out of their birdfeeders. The easiest solution to this is to rename it a squirrel and bird feeder. A savvy person will try to see objections and roadblocks in advance and plot a pathway around them beforehand. Sometimes it is not possible to do this. Sometimes technology or policies have not yet caught up with what the project entails. Sometimes you just have to wait and sometimes things are not possible at all, not at that time or at that institution. Then it is best to set that project or goal aside, move on, and return to it later.

One simple item is a name. While a rose by any other name may smell as sweet, it is easier to discuss that particular rose with other rose sniffers if the rose has a standard, agreed upon name. So should people. Call yourself whatever you wish in your personal life but professionally it is easier, especially in a publishing environment, to use just one name, and just one form of that name. I did not change my name when I married. My children have my husband's surname. In parenting situations I am frequently called Mrs. Husbandsname. I answer to that very pleasantly, but at work I am always Julie Still. Here again people (and this is usually women) will have to make their own decisions. A man who marries, divorces, and remarries, leaves no trace of these changes in his name; a woman with the same history could have a total of three surnames in one workplace (first married name, return to maiden name, second married name). That just gets a little complicated. We all know how troublesome it is when serial publications change name; it is the same with people. I have not always been consistent in the use of a middle initial, something I now regret as it makes tracking citation analysis more difficult. Pick a formal name for publication and stick with it. A man named Timothy may be Timmy to family, and Tim to friends, but he should choose one of those three as his presentation and publication name and use it consistently.

The path to tenure most often has a guidebook, a contract or some other document that spells out what steps need to be taken and what needs to be accomplished to meet the minimum requirements. If an institution has such a document someone wanting tenure should sit down and read it front to back, cover to cover, and take notes. This is the map. Is there an interim step or steps? Is the initial contract for a set number of years to be renewed for an additional year or years? This is important knowledge to have. Does the contract explain what areas are required? The usual divisions are teaching (librarianship), research, and service. Does the contract explain how they are weighed? Is it equally or does one count for more than another? Are there exceptions to any of these rules? Some places offer the possibility of an extension for new parents or for health reasons. This is important to know.

Words on paper have meaning. The shades of meaning between verbs proceeded by "can," "should," and "will" can have a tremendous impact on how situations play out. For example, a statement that "new parents can be allowed a year out of the tenure stream" is different from "new parents should be allowed a year out of the tenure stream" and both of those are far less assured than "new parents will be allowed a year out of the tenure stream." Read carefully over the regulations, guidelines, and policies. If they refer to other documents those should be located and read as well. Many contracts allow for appeal under very specific circumstances. Perhaps only the process can be appealed. This can only be successful if the candidate knows what the process is and if it was followed. A lapse on the part of the candidate could annul any appeal. Hopefully it would never come to that, but having one's I's dotted and T's crossed can avoid problems later on should there be any questions. Also try to find out what current practice has been regarding the written rules. What have people been doing as far as family leave? While work at home is allowed according to the rules, is it done in practice? While the tenure guidelines do not specify what kind of publications are needed what have recent successful applicants been doing? This sort of inquiry is best done delicately, by observation at first and then by subtle questions.

Another aspect of the tenure process is the organizational structure. Who makes the decisions? How are those people selected or are only certain people designated as the decision makers? If you have the information available see who has and has not gotten tenure lately. Does one part of the organization have a better record of getting people tenured than another? Are there reasons for that?

How is the tenure packet prepared? Are there standard forms to be filled out? Who fills out what part? What are the responsibilities of the applicant? Are letters of support required? From whom? What kinds of supporting documentation are required?

What is the timeline? Note when paperwork is due and when decisions are made. Note when everyone's materials are due and to whom. There are delicate ways to nudge colleagues and deans to ensure that packets are delivered to the proper office by the deadline. Department heads and directors nominally have responsibility for getting things to the proper office, but it is the candidate's job on the line, so it behooves that person to make sure, even if in a gingerly fashion, that something was not forgotten or that the envelope got put in the correct mail bin. If someone has offered to drive or hand carry the packet to the place it needs to go, find some way of making sure that person was not sick that day. While there is often some leeway in deadlines no one really wants their tenure packet to start off requesting an exception.

What is the process itself like? Who makes the final decision and how many individuals or bodies does the packet go through? Often there is a department decision (in large institutions there may be several stops along the way, the department, the department head, the school, and the school's tenure committee) and then, if the packet is cleared at that level, an institutional decision. There are unlikely to be any librarians on the institutional tenure committee. You cannot assume that they have ever spoken to a librarian. Who decides who sits on what committee? Are positions elected or appointed? Can you find out who is on the committee and how long those people will be there? The decision process for an interim contract renewal may be different from the tenure process; again, it is important to know this.

If at all possible see if copies of recent successful packets are available. Copies may be kept in the institution's human resources department or recently tenured colleagues may loan out a copy of their packet. This is very helpful in seeing how the official guidelines relate to actual performance. It is advisable to look at as many packets as possible. What did they have in common? What differed among them? If you can see the letters of support look at how many letters each person had and where they were from. Internal letters are more likely to be public than external letters, the ones from people outside the university. Take a note of how many letters there are for each aspect of the person's job and what sort of things did they say. Look for patterns, what is there, as well as, what is not. What kind of physical packaging is used (Notebooks? Dividers? Sheet covers, yes or no?). It is impossible to have too much information in this regard. If no recent packets are available think about why this might be. Is it because no one has gone up for tenure recently? Is it a place where everyone has been tenured for a long time and there was a recent retirement? Have several people gone up for tenure, but none successfully (this is concerning)? Have people been tenured, but there is not a cultural practice of sharing information (this is also concerning)?

Many tenure processes require outside letters, also called external reviewers. Someone, usually human resources or the tenure committee, will send requests to experts or established scholars in your field asking them to provide an opinion on your work. This can be the scariest part of tenure. It is important to know if your institution uses outside letters and, if so, who decides who those people will be. Find out if you can make recommendations and how closely those recommendations will be followed. Can they be people you have served on committees with? If your areas of specialty are small it is impossible to find people who do not know you. More common areas of focus will provide a wider pool or reviewers. Throughout the pre-tenure years you can be on the lookout for potential reviewers. Find out if reviewers need to be from peer institutions or if they have to be at institutions that have tenured librarians. If someone who can give a good overview of your work is outside those parameters you may still be able to include them if you can give a good rationale. Perhaps they write in your field frequently or have held office in an organization that you are active in. Also find out if you can ask that people not be an outside reviewer. Perhaps someone wrote a bad review of one of your publications or you ran against each other for office and it left bad feelings on their part. All of this is important information to know. Clemons and Goldberg have written an excellent overview of external reviews in the library promotion and tenure process.

Once this information is on hand, create a document that can be updated or where notes can be taken. This can be a physical document or a digital space, but it should be a representation of all that is needed to reach the destination. List the categories, list the items needed. If tenure requires a mix of the standard teaching/librarianship, scholarship/research, and service, then create three categories and list any specifics or ideas from previous successful packets. Is there an emphasis on single-authored peer review journal articles? Note that. Is a certain level of service the norm? Do people usually have a mix of local, state, national involvement in professional associations? Is service in alternate organizations allowed? Note that as well. This is the basic space to be used in planning out one's strategy. Not everyone has to follow the same path, but knowing past practices allows a skillful tenure candidate to craft a packet so that their actions, even if different from that of other recent applicants, are presented in a similar enough fashion that the committees can relate to and understand them.

Going from point A to point B does not always involve the straightest route. Sometimes there are mountains to go around which involves a longer route, but beautiful scenery. Sometimes the road is bumpy and the journey not that pleasant. Sometimes a planned route is interrupted by detours and new maps have to be created. A change in marital status or the addition of children or elderly parents can mean that traveling or flexible schedules are no longer as easy as they once were. Health issues crop up that require the development of new habits or other life changes. New hires at work whose skill set lets them fill a void that you had wanted to work towards, or, conversely, a void opens and you shift/are shifted into it when you might have had other plans.

The theory of evolution tell us that a species has three basic options when faced with changed circumstances: adapt, migrate, or die out. Societies and cultures are the same. Assuming the last option is undesirable, that leaves adapt or migrate. Adaptation might mean setting aside a project or a goal for at least a short time, or seeking an avenue for personal fulfillment on a specific area elsewhere, outside the job; it might mean learning new skills needed as job changes or learning to adjust to coworkers who view the world differently. Migration might mean a shift to a different department or a different job at the same institution or a new job altogether.

There are times when travelers change their destination midway and decide to go off in a different direction entirely. This may be by choice or circumstance. Parents of special needs children sometimes describe having such children as planning a journey to Italy and landing in Holland instead. There is nothing wrong with Holland, it just is not where they intended to go. So they learn to make the best of it. Another story that illustrates this point is the urban legend known as "the naval carrier and the lighthouse." One night a large navy vessel sees another light ahead and calls for what it presumes is another ship to change its course to avoid a collision. A voice from the other light tells the ship to change its course. They go back and forth a bit with the captain of the ship calling out the size or intent or mission of his ship and demanding the other ship move first. The voice at the other light calls back finally and said "This is the lighthouse." The gist being that sometimes we have to change our course. Very few people grew up wanting to be librarians, though perhaps in retrospect it seems inevitable. Things happen, dreams change. Sometimes very lofty goals are significantly simplified; other times unexpected vistas open up and opportunities we have never dreamt of show up on our doorsteps. Sometimes you find yourself at a given place and decide that this is where you were headed all along.

Routes get changed for a number of reasons, but it remains important to create a map, and then change it if needed. Starting out without a map at all will doubtless lead to circular routes with no destination, or no chance of reaching the intended destination.

We find ourselves on pathways that were not what we originally intended, but once there it is a good idea to come up with some sort of game plan. Where are we heading? What do we want? What is the best way to get there? Maps and lists of goals and priorities are elastic documents; they change. However, it is important to have something to start with. In the next chapter of this book, we will set up ways of checking progress along the route.

Counting your assets

3

Equipped with a destination and a map, now our traveler must weigh what she has and what she needs. Taking stock is like looking at a recipe, seeing what ingredients are needed, going through the pantry to see what is on hand, and then watching for opportunities to pick up the remaining ingredients. Counting one's assets is never a completed process. New assets are added all the time. In the last chapter, readers created a list of what was required to reach the destination. In this chapter, we start trying to meet those goals. If the last chapter involved developing a personal mission statement, this chapter involves creating a strategic plan.

For any endeavor, the most important asset or resource is time. Money is often mentioned as well but in many ways it is secondary. Note that the verbs used to describe time are the same ones used to describe money. We spend both. We save both. We invest both. We squander both. However, money can sit idle, time never does. Time passes whether we will use it or not. Money can be replenished but time cannot. It is imperative to mention this. Tenure clocks tick away in a ruthless manner. Time passes whether it is saved or squandered. Twenty-four hours of it disappears every day, never to be had again. Time is an untenured person's most valuable asset.

Beware of those who would be cavalier with it. Friendly chats in the office are great team building or mentoring opportunities, but a daily gossip session is unproductive and the time could be put to much better use. The Japanese language includes a phrase, arigata meiwaku, which means an unwanted favor someone has done for you and for which you must express gratitude. A colleague's well-intentioned effort may end up being more trouble than it was worth. This can come in the form of being on a committee that takes up a lot of time but produces very little. It may be an invitation to participate in a research project with someone who has a poor completion record, or to help plan an event that seems unlikely to occur. It is flattering if someone who wants your opinion or to run an unformed idea past you, but not if you are on deadline with another project. An easy out here is to say "I'd love to talk about that with you but I have to finish this report today. Can we meet tomorrow to talk this over? I'd be able to focus on it better then." Some people can solve a problem better by working through it aloud than by thinking it over quietly. They will often look for someone to act as the sounding board, whose primary purpose in this exchange is to listen. This is wonderful for the first person, but not so wonderful for the second person, who has invested an equal amount of time but receives little in return.

While the saying "do unto others as you would have them do unto you" is an admirable one it does not necessarily mean to do for others what you want done, but do for others what they would like done. For example, someone who does not like surprise parties, but is friends with someone who does should take into account. It is important to understand not only how co-workers approach issues and problems, but to have enough self-awareness to understand how we ourselves approach them. Knowing how we work best and striving to arrange a work pattern that implements that, and in the process inconveniencing others as little as possible is an important step toward a successful career. Above all else a newly hired librarian or academic, especially in a tenure setting, must have good time management skills. Know what time of the day you are most productive and guard that for high-priority items or those requiring the most focus and concentration. It is also important to know our own weaknesses, what we might unwittingly do to sabotage ourselves. Any chronic health condition needs to be managed; a week in the hospital due to neglecting a few hours preventive care is a week lost. A day in court to handle those parking tickets you ignored is a day lost. If you know that you are likely to fret about an upcoming deadline, but not actually do the work until the last minute, make sure you can set aside time when the deadline is upon you and work on secondary tasks until then, so entire days or weeks are not lost to avoidance behaviors.

Any activity that can serve two purposes at once should do so. I use public transit to get to and from work and while train time often serves as a way to relax after work and prepare for the home front, it is also time to read, catch up on the news, check email, and so on. Before the advent of smart phones I would use this time exclusively for reading; to increase the value of this I signed up to write book reviews for a magazine aimed at collection development librarians. Since the magazine tried to match up reviewers' interests and backgrounds with the titles they sent out, I was reading books that I enjoyed. While it was relaxing, it also provided me with a series of lower level publications. In the chapter on research, we will discuss further ways to integrate not only work-related projects, but also personal interests into publications and presentations.

Knowledge is another general asset. The two best ways to acquire it are reading and direct experience. For people who have taken a job in a new town and have not yet built social connections, there is no better way to spend an evening than reading. Read everything, read all the time. It need not be work related. Outside interests come in to play here as well as they did in the first chapter. And just as important, find a way of recording what is read. Whether in paper or in digital form or online keep some form of reading log. This might be a way to use social media, if this is the information you want to make public, or use online tools that you can keep private. Keep a correct citation and any notes of interest about the item, including a notation of anything intriguing in the bibliography. This is more easily done for books. Not every article needs to be noted, but those that are particularly interesting should be recorded in some way. Those who enjoy films or music should keep notes on those as well. Any activity that leads to new knowledge should be tracked in some form. Papers written in graduate school (challenging undergraduate papers as well) are an asset.

Personal contacts are an asset. This is not to mean that people should be befriended for the sole reason that they might later be of use, but everyone knows someone. Professional networking sites, such as LinkedIn and Academia are ways to maintain work-related (and personal) connections. There are ways of maintaining professional connections without the pretense of interpersonal affection. Use of more general social media, such as Facebook will frequently mingle the professional and personal; people will need to make individual decisions on whether or not to combine the two. Some, when a work colleague asks to connect on a form of social media they use solely for personal reasons, will ask if they can connect on a professional site instead. In general, any form of social media that involves professional contacts should avoid controversial topics, unless that particular topic ties in to your job. There are any number of tales of people who lost a job because they were indiscrete on social media. It is easy to forget, typing away alone in the evening or the early morning hours, that once you hit the send button the entire world can see what you have written. Networking is a skill that can be developed. It pertains not only to professional contacts, but also to those personal connections we make through hobbies, civic engagement, and other activities. In the previous chapter, the importance of activities outside of work was mentioned. The people one encountered there are also assets.

Organizational abilities are not just an asset, but an absolute requirement for tenure. Shoes go in the shoe basket by the door, keys on the key hook, and glasses in a specific place every day. The gas tank never gets below a quarter full. Many an opportunity is lost or squandered because we could not find our keys or had to stop for gas or we did not have quarters for the meter or money for a stamp. Solid organizational skills are often the difference between success and failure. Juggling multiple roles in life or just juggling multiple responsibilities in the workplace means that things are often done on deadline or at the last minute. It is often simply the way of things. However, sound preparation, or at least overall readiness is essential. This means making sure the ink-jets in the printer would not run out, or if they do that a fresh cartridge is available, that clothes are set out the night before or at least that laundry is done, that documents are filed in such a way that they are findable. The morning rush, exacerbated by a cat that spit up or the need to sing another song for the baby, is smoothed if the agenda and paperwork needed for the morning meeting had been printed out the night before and are sitting on the desk. The missed lunch on a harried day is replaced by a quick granola bar or can of emergency soup stored in the office. Ask others for tips. One colleague with several children told me she simplified the laundry by buying white tube socks for everyone. There was no worry about matching socks or deciding who had whose socks. Everyone's socks were the same and kept in a tub on the landing. Each morning every child picked up two white socks. This may not work for everyone, but it made one small aspect of her life very easy. I adopted that same plan as long as my children allowed it. The person in the household responsible for meal preparation usually has some organizational system. I keep a grocery list on the refrigerator. As people within the household learned to read and write they were taught to add items to the grocery list. Eat the last chip? Add it to the list. Running low on a favorite cereal? Add it to the list. If it is not on the list do not assume it will be bought. Another mother puts the week's menu plans on the refrigerator along with the needed ingredients. Anything on that list cannot be eaten for a snack, or else the family will be having soup on the night that an ingredient has already been eaten. It sounds regimented, but unless someone in the house can go to the grocery store at the last minute or the household can afford to eat, take out, or delivery on a regular basis, lists like that are a must. A hectic life can still be a well-ordered life and, as will be a theme in this book, a moment of advance preparation can free up hours later.

In general, though, what is meant by tracking one's assets is noting accomplishments. This does not mean just degrees earned or items published, but a list of all of one's accomplishments. Skills and abilities, knowledge bases, people one knows, are all assets. Completed committee work is an asset. Informal reports and working papers are assets. Policy statements are assets. They are all things to draw upon for future endeavors.

3.1 Measurement without judgment

There is a natural tendency to assign value to things and characteristics. Granted some things are inherently larger than others, but different tools are needed at different times. Scalpels and sledgehammers both fulfill a purpose, as do tweezers and the Jaws of Life. Knowing what is in the toolbox means not dismissing some things out of hand. Women especially can denigrate or downplay their accomplishments or not recognize them as accomplishments. In tracking one's assets it is important to track everything. As an example, most people take at least a few classes in another language while in college, not necessarily by choice—it is often a requirement. This introduction, even if only one or two semesters, is an asset. One might assume that within a library there would be several people with some knowledge of any one particular language, but that may not be so. Someone's two semesters of German may make them the in-house expert by virtue of being the only person who has had any training in it at all. Growing up with an immigrant granny who sang lullabies in her native Japanese may well make that person the in-house expert on that language. A familiarity with online games is an asset. Spending some hours a week playing Minecraft may not seem like an asset-building activity, but if there is a question about it or if the library is asked to contribute to a campus discussion on whether or not to create a game-like activity for students, the person with the most experience becomes the local expert. As the old saying goes, in the land of the blind the one-eyed man is the king.

While a tenure packet needs hefty accomplishments it also needs a few smaller things to balance out the presentation. A plate with just steak on it might be filling, but a side dish or sprig of parsley makes it much more appealing. A colorful salad would really brighten up the plate. A series of small book reviews makes a nice small side dish or garnish. Sometimes the small things can make a big difference, so the items or accomplishments that seem insignificant could play a much larger role in the grand scheme.

We seldom examine our own activities with a clinical eye, but it is important to understand what skills and attributes we have, and on tenure track all of them are likely to be needed at one point or another. That was alluded to in the previous chapter, but it should also be noted here. Work style and personal preferences are assets, though not always applicable to every situation.

A simple initial way of measuring one's assets is to simply make a list of definitive accomplishments, degrees, certificates, classes and workshops taken (and taught), job skills, publications and presentations, committees and organizations that you have been or are active in, graduate school papers that still have any relevance, outside hobbies and activities (present and former), and so on. Nothing is too small or too insignificant. The list of books and notable articles read is a part of this, but should be in a separate document. The asset list will grow, diminish, and change as time goes on.

Viewing something in a negative light should not prevent it from being put on the asset list. An article that was not accepted at one (or more) publications is simply a manuscript that can be sent out on short notice to another publishing opportunity. An unpleasant encounter with someone may be the opening salvo in a relationship with someone else who has also had an unpleasant encounter with that person. Being pushed out of an organization, or leaving after butting heads with the leader, is an opportunity to start anew with a different organization. Having received a D in a college statistics class is still light years ahead of someone who has no familiarity with statistics at all. Everything is relative.

3.2   Discrete pieces of information

Socrates said the unexamined life is not worth living. He had a point. Taking stock of one's life is not always pleasant, but it is essential. This is especially true for people on tenure track. Think of each individual item as a building block or Lego. Some are larger than others, but all are building materials. Some will be obvious—degrees, certificates, and language ability; others will be more difficult to tease out. Graduate (or even well-written undergraduate) papers are an asset. Each committee served on is an asset.

As one example of separating out discrete pieces of information, serving on a committee brings in several types of assets. One is the actual work of the committee and what it accomplishes or produces. A second would be contacts made due to work on the committee, who else was on it and what their jobs or roles are. A third asset would be any news skills learned while working on the committee, software used, background material read. Every activity produces a number of assets. Any written acknowledgement of the committee work is also an asset. It is very helpful to keep some record of these items, otherwise it is difficult to recall, especially a few years down the road, the who, what, and where. Sometimes an old-fashioned file folder for each committee or project can be helpful.

Working with a gift collection or selecting library materials for a new program brings in new assets, enhanced knowledge of the subject area, connections with people in that area, and the physical assets themselves. Investigating possible purchases or adoption of a new or different software product or tool produces not only the item itself (if selected), but added knowledge of the item and others similar to it, contact with any people consulted, either at the vendor or others who use that item, and assorted paperwork.

Even failures can be an asset. Everything is a learning experience. Sometimes we learn that we are not good at particular jobs; this allows us to focus interests elsewhere. A stint as acting director may change an ambition to move into management. That allows the person to find ways of being more integral to the institution in other ways. A project attempted that does not come to fruition may still be a way of learning new skills.

3.3   Tools for tracking activity

The scenario mentioned at the beginning of this book, of the librarian sitting down the night before her tenure packet is due and asking "What have I done the last five years?" is completely avoidable. Everyone, in any position, needs to have some record keeping mechanism for their daily or overall productivity. This can be as simple as a calendar with notations on meetings, project status, and a to do list. It can be a series of spreadsheet pages. Some who work primarily over an email will use a series of folders or tags to track projects. Others use a more complex system. Virtually every book or article I read in preparation for writing this book mentioned the importance of organization and documentation. Spires (2007) follows much the same system that I do (daily log, monthly report, and folders). Miller, McDonald, and Jia (2005) says the best advice she received was the importance of documentation.

Organization is important to tracking activity. The stereotypic image of someone being audited taking a shoebox full of receipts to the IRS office is, sadly, all too often accurate. Simply keeping things is not always helpful. They need to be kept in some order. For instance, librarians on tenure track will have, hopefully by this time, read over the tenure documents and any relevant work contract, and will know what areas they will need to demonstrate competence or mastery in for tenure, or what accomplishments are required. In the previous chapter there was a suggestion to create a document listing the requirements for tenure or contract renewal, or simply meeting personal goals. The tracking mechanism should mirror these categories. If the standard division of librarianship/teaching, scholarship/research, and service apply then that is how activity should be recorded. It is also important to take into account short-term and long-term goals.

How are each of these categories measured? Scholarship and service are fairly straightforward, but there are subtleties which will be discussed in later chapters. The ways librarianship is measured depends on the job description or subject area involved. Each of the three main areas would be measured somewhat differently and the specifics of each are gone over in detail in subsequent chapters. However, as a starting exercise, it is a good idea to construct a measurement mechanism. A public services librarian will undoubtedly have assigned public contact hours of one or more kinds: reference desk hours, emails, online reference, online chat service, and so on. Those hours should be counted. Most public service librarians will do some form of instruction. This also should be counted (and noted by subject area). A technical services librarian will monitor her workflow, whether it is the number of books cataloged or the problem tickets resolved or digital collections added or managed. A librarian in systems will record problems solved, systems upgrades, and new systems learned.

These are the items that will eventually populate a tenure document or provide the support for a promotion packet or the cover letter for a new job. These are the items that will build the bridge to a new area of career growth. Knowing who you are and what you do provides a bulwark against the chaos of the world. Institutions often have strategic plans. Tying accomplishments and assets to those plans will show an adherence to institutional goals and provide excellent fodder for tenure or promotion narratives.

A librarian who wants to eventually go into management will want to track career items that are related to management, such as committees chaired, supervisory activities, prominent roles in larger organizations, and so on. A librarian who knows that her job will shift in a few years due to impending technology changes will track items in a way that moves toward the new workflow, for example, someone in serials who sees that print subscriptions are phasing out as online packages become more popular will more closely track items relating to the digital world. Simply tracking these items helps keep focused on the goal.

There are intangibles as well. If a job is heavily dependent on interaction with one or more groups of people then any form of acknowledgement from them should be kept in some way. Not all will be needed, but it is useful to have a selection to choose from. Anyone wanting to go into management might want to track how many people come to them for advice or consultation on professional matters. If anyone voluntarily sends a "thanks, that was helpful" email or note, it, also, should be kept. Someone who wants to eventually move into collection development might note how many potential book donors he or she talks with and what the result is.

Whatever tracking method an individual chooses, he or she needs to keep it up to date. Set aside time at the end of a day or week or even month, to collect up the data from that time period. As previously mentioned, I take public transit and on the way home note the events of the day in a blank journal book, any public service hours, classes, interactions with students or faculty, projects worked on, meetings attended, and so on. At the end of every month these activities are collected and noted on a one page report. The report is a template based on the three standard categories: librarianship (public service hours, instruction, interactions with liaison students and faculty, collection development, and job-related committees), scholarship (projects worked on, publications, and proposals sent out any status updates—accepted or rejected), and service (committee meetings, organization activities, and work-related community activities). Emails from that month are reviewed and deleted, noteworthy emails, especially those acknowledging work, involvement or assistance, printed out and attached to the report. At the end of the year it is easy to assemble an annual report, simply by compiling the twelve monthly reports. It takes a little time each day and about an hour each month, but it saves a lot of time at the end of the year (Still, 2005). The categories in the monthly report shift from year to year as job duties shift and as career goals shift, but the format of the reporting document remains the same. There are high-tech versions of this system, online cloud-based note keeping systems or electronic calendaring systems, which will allow categorizations or color coding. Each individual will find their own best practice or preferred technology. For me it is easier to do in a Word document, each year kept in a separate file with a new page for each month, printed out and filed in a folder close at hand in or near my desk. Letters and other documentation are tucked in easily. At the end of the year that file goes into a file drawer farther away.

The librarian referenced at the beginning of this book, who was sitting down to put together a tenure packet and could not recall what she had done during her five years at the institution would have been saved by simple record keeping. If tenure is not a goal, being able to demonstrate how one has justified a salary, and why, if there are job reductions, one has been productive is common sense. There are also times when files like this can serve as institutional memory—when was a certain committee active, what did it do, when was a particular project completed, search committee formed, and so on. Being able to quickly review that sort of data can be very valuable to an organization.

When a tenure committee or merit raise committee is sitting around a table reviewing documentation from eligible librarians they can only consider what is in front of them. A candidate might have worked on an important project or been the guiding light for a new service or system upgrade, but the committee cannot consider that if it is not on the paperwork submitted. A poorly documented packet can be heartbreaking for everyone: both the candidate, and the committee whose members know that the person they are evaluating has done more, but those items are not referenced. When a packet is still in draft form it can be revised, but once it is handed in it is usually a finished, unalterable document. A colleague might review a draft and say "you should include X or Y," but once the door is closed and the committee deliberates that option is likely no longer available. It is neither collegial nor neighborly to put friends and co-workers in the position of being our keeper. People should know what they do and how they contribute to the whole. Keeping good records will lead to producing a good packet.

This is also often true of merit raises, non-tenure related promotion, and other kinds of formal work assessment. It cannot be assumed that everyone understands what any particular job entails or how it is done. These evaluations are the time to tell that story. How long did it take to do a particular project, what was involved? How does it fit into overall framework of the library, or the campus?

Record keeping is not just for the past, but also for the future. One file that everyone should have is a "possibilities" folder, whether it is an actual manila folder hanging in a file cabinet or an online link list. This is the place to put calls for papers, conference announcements, requests for volunteers, grant listings, program notes, mentions of intriguing committees, and so on. Also note the deadline for these and whether it is a one-time opportunity or something that comes around on a regular or semi-regular basis. These things are too easily lost or forgotten or overlooked. Having such a folder and reviewing it frequently will provide for a much greater scope of opportunity.

3.4   Circles of colleagues

While the saying "it's not what you know it's who you know," has definite value, the corollary, "it's not who you know but who the people you know know" is just as apt. Jobs are more likely found via connections of connections than from people we directly know. We find jobs or good used cars or hand me down maternity clothes or people to talk with our child's scout troop from people like our significant other's next door neighbor or a child's friend's older sister's boss's son. The father of the younger girl your daughter walks home with teaches a class on art law and makes a great addition to a panel program on intellectual property. The circulation desk supervisor's brother will hire your son to help him do landscaping work over the summer. It is the wider circles, the connections of connections, that will prove to be most valuable.

One of the more stressful aspects of tenure is finding people to write letters. Most institutions require outside letters, from people at other institutions, to comment on the scholarship and service of the tenure candidate. New and untenured librarians might think they do not know anyone to suggest, and in truth most of the people they know are likely to be untenured librarians as well. However, the wider circles of contacts will often provide possible reviewers. If untenured librarian A will be going up for tenure, she can ask tenured colleagues for suggestions on outside reviewers. She can also contact untenured librarian B and ask if any of the tenured librarians there would be suitable. She can look at the professional associations she has been involved with and see who she knows there might be a good reviewer, or contact committee chairs and see if they have any recommendations.

As mentioned earlier, it is important to have a life outside of work. The people met and interacted with in those settings are another circle. An alumni network is another circle. These kinds of linkages can be a challenge for the introverted or the shy but a pleasant, friendly demeanor can go a long way toward keeping in contact even if small talk is not a skill. Po Bronson, author of *What Should I Do With My Life*, was asked how to avoid burnout. He talked about having a life outside of work:

> *An enormous amount of my time goes to my family, my kids, my volunteer work as a youth soccer coach. I get energy from those parts of my life, and that makes me better at what I do professionally. Spend time with people outside of your field but in related fields, at conferences or socially. New ways of thinking will energize you.*
>
> Rosato (2013).

Getting outside of an occupational bubble also helps people stay connected with the larger population. People who work at a college or university sometimes lose sight of how the rest of the population thinks. Working in an information technology-rich area can lead to the worldview that everyone knows how to use the Internet and other information tools. That bubble is burst when working with a community group and trying to set up an email distribution list that everyone can use. As of this writing a Google Group or a Yahoo Group are some of the ways to do that, something that seems quite simple, but for participants to whom such technologies are new and alarming the whole process is daunting, if even possible. Trying to help scout families register their daughter in Girl Scouts when the organization went to online as opposed to paper registration was another eye opener. Even in an information society there are large parts of the general populace that do not engage with technology in the ways we think they might. Interacting with a larger world helps us to be more empathetic with students or colleagues who are technologically challenged. It also reminds us that presentations to a wider audience need to be more inclusive, to understand that not everyone will understand our acronyms or jargon.

Registering with professional social media, such as the aforementioned LinkedIn or Academia.edu is a big help with networking. Over time the number of contacts grows. When reaching out to vendors or librarians at other institutions for work-related reasons, it is perfectly acceptable to ask "May I connect with you on LinkedIn?" Other forms of social media are of varying usefulness. Having 500 twitter followers is great if the twitter feed is somehow connected to work and if the 500 followers are in a variety of positions that connect with one's current job or a desired future job. Being unemployed and having 500 also unemployed twitter followers is not necessarily a good pathway to finding a job. Fellow tweeps might send around job notes or mention possibilities they themselves are not interested in, but a group of people all competing for the same jobs may not be the best place to network. As, or if, those people find jobs they might be in a position to suggest your name for committee spots in professional organizations or let you know of any openings they hear about, but new hires generally have little influence at their institution. Potential employers looking at that twitter feed might not be impressed if it appears to be a bubble where people speak only to each other, but do so in a public forum for all to see. However, saying at an interview that you have experience on social media and helped the library build a following from students and faculty should be mentioned as an asset during interviews; but there should be evidence that your work would be positive and reflect well on the institution. Calling attention to a blog that frequently includes complaints is not likely to help in a job interview setting. Spending several hours a day on Facebook to talk with fellow high school classmates who live on the other side of the country is helpful in finding restaurants if a conference is being held there, but it might interfere with other job duties and perhaps that amount of time should be reduced.

The depth and breadth of engagement with circles of colleagues will ebb and flow, and while it is always a good practice to be polite and considerate, the time pressures of tenure will have some impact on the amount of time that is spent with each circle. An active life outside of work is, as has been mentioned, important, vital even, but it might be more time with fewer people or a deeper investment with fewer groups. This is a delicate balance with the positive and negative aspects weighed and re-weighed on a regular basis.

Getting out of the library and having a life outside of work is also important for another reason—it allows others to see you. I try to attend public events hosted by my state representative, state senator, and congressional representative each year. It is not so much that I need to see them, but that they see me and recognize that their constituents are involved and concerned. You may be the only librarian or public employee or college employee that your circle of colleagues knows. This concept was reinforced for me when I was involved in a community project that brought me in contact with the township commissioners where I live. One worked in the finance office of a college and called me one afternoon to ask me about the way libraries paid vendors as he had questions about some invoices and did not understand how that relationship worked and how electronic resources were priced. He did not call me because he thought I was an expert at this. He called me because I was the only librarian he knew. In our non-work lives we will often be in this situation and our ability to translate our work to those who are not familiar with it can make a difference in how people vote on bond issues and how they respond to public initiatives on libraries and higher education.

Just getting out of the library within our home institution will help build up campus or organizational networks. What does it say if the public library director is the only city department head who does not attend city council meetings? What happens if campus administrators never see a librarian? As mentioned before about town hall forums, I go to them not just so that I can see my elected officials, but so they can see me. Likewise, I attend campus meetings not only so that I can see liaison faculty and talk with administrators and staff, but so they can see me, and note that librarians are part of the organizational fabric. It is just as, or more, important to be seen than to see.

3.5 Working with people

The importance of focusing on goals was discussed in the previous chapter. That focus is especially helpful when working in groups. There is an old saying "There is no end to what you can accomplish if you do not mind who gets the credit." This is very true, and something to definitely keep in mind when working toward tenure. If a dean is the person who can green light a project then does it matter if the dean is a bit tedious or arrogant, provided the green light is given? Does it matter if the dean is praised for developing the idea? (This is hypothetical—I work with lovely deans.) The willingness of elected officials to partner with people it is clear they do not like and have previously publicly disparaged is often seen as a character flaw. In truth, they are often doing whatever it takes to bring jobs or positive media to their district. Two men who, before an election were on opposite sides and denounced each other in interviews or one disparaged the other in favor of an opponent, will breakfast together the next day. "Spineless," people will say, but those two men will now represent some of the same citizens and geographic areas and if they want to bring infrastructure improvements to those areas they will have to work together. Sharing credit or thanking people for help that they may not in fact have provided is a way of letting them feel some pride of ownership in your accomplishments and gaining their support for your projects.

When preparing tenure or promotion packets it is vital to present yourself as part of a team, even if you do not always feel that way. Acknowledge the assistance of your colleagues in your narrative using wording that does not seem incongruous with the rest of your work or sound as if it were hastily stuck in. For instance you might say "as part of a vital reference department I was active in providing public service in a variety of ways" or "my colleagues provided a supportive work environment that has allowed me to focus on research" or "with the guidance of the library administration I embarked on a digitization project." Remember that at least some of your colleagues will be reading your packet and you do not want to alienate them at that particular juncture. You did not spring into existence fully formed, as Athena did from Zeus's head. Your colleagues had the sense to hire you and, if nothing else, give you space and stay out of your way. Chances are they answered your questions and helped you settle in. Someone provided you with an orientation to your workplace, saw to it that you had access to paper, pens, and made sure your computer was working. This may seem like a given, but remember how many award show speeches thank spouses, partners, parents, and teachers. Even though parents are supposed to provide safe housing, adequate meals, and hopefully emotional support, it remains no less true that our existence is heavily dependent upon that. We still send them cards and call on Mother's Day and Father's Day. If you are in a challenging environment you have learned something, even if it is how to dodge bullets and jump through hoops. A tenure or promotion packet, once it has left the library, in some ways represents the entire body of librarians. As much as possible keep it upbeat and collegial. If you, like me, have worked with colleagues who have gone out of their way to smooth your path, it is important to acknowledge that in this public forum.

It is said that people may not remember what you say, they may not remember what you do, but they will always remember how you made them feel. Therefore it is important, as much as possible, to have people think well of you. Simply saying "thank you" or "that is very helpful" or "that is certainly something to think about" lets the other person walk away feeling useful, involved, and respected, even if they have not been any of those things. This has not gone out of style simply because we have entered the digital age. Early in their book *The Complete Social Media Community Manager's Guide*, Marty Weintraub and Lauren Litwinka write "The finest way to earn likes is to model likable behavior and not be a jerk" (Weintraub & Litwinka, 2013, p. 36). This is good advice all around. At some point everyone has literal or figurative toilet paper on their shoe. If you have not been nice to the people around you they may not tell you that your slip is showing, your blouse has lost a button, your zipper is down, or that the report you are about to turn in has an embarrassing typo in it. They are not obligated to do so; it is incumbent upon you to create a situation where they will do so willingly.

There is sometimes a sense that being busy all the time is a sign of importance. That is not necessarily so. People who can prioritize and work strategically more often appear calm, confident, and competent. Those who are constantly rushing or overly busy can actually create what is called "second hand stress" in their colleagues (Shellenbarger, 2013). They can make others feel anxious and inferior, and engender resentment. A colleague with a legitimate question may have to track the busy person down or chase them through the halls to get an answer; eventually colleagues will simply avoid that person. In the end, they did not do themselves any favor by being so frenetic.

When working on a project it is easy for things to fall between the cracks. If someone considers the success of that project a goal then it is incumbent upon that person to follow through. These scenarios are examples:

- Susan asks Maria if she would be interested in working on a campus committee. Maria says yes and assumes that ends the matter, that she will be on the committee. As it turns out Susan is not putting together the committee, she overheard Andrea and Bob talking about it and thought Maria would be a good addition, but she forgets to tell Andrea or Bob. If being on that committee is important to Maria she should have asked Susan if she should follow-up with anyone, and Maria should certainly look for opportunities to remind Susan about the offer or to touch base with Andrea or Bob.
- In a planning meeting, Tina says that Patrick is the person who can provide a needed service. Louann assumes that Tina will follow-up with Patrick. Tina assumes that Louann will. Louann sees Patrick at a reception and mentions it to him thinking this will take care of things. Patrick waits for a formal written request that neither woman sends him. Patrick assumes it was a passing matter and does not arrange for the service. No one follows up with Patrick. The service is not provided.

• Mike tells Joanna that Twyla needs help with a project. Joanna arranges her time to do so and then touches base with Twyla short before the project. It turns out that Mike had not talked with Twyla and Twyla does not need help. Joanna should have contacted Twyla immediately to find out from her what she wanted before taking any action.

These triangulations and dropped connections are a prime cause of the gridlock and frustration. It is important to find out who is the person to contact about specific areas and arrange for who will contact that person. Follow-up is vital. For ongoing projects repeated follow-up is required.

That leads in part to a discussion of institutional culture. Every new hire is dropped into a pre-existing ecosystem, with unwritten rules and rituals. Some places have a very hierarchical structure; others are more democratic. There may be diversity of opinion on professional or personal matters or it could be a very homogeneous environment. Many groups, whether they may be families, workplaces, organizations, or groups of friends will have what is sometimes called a "missing stair." In houses there is often a flaw that is time consuming or otherwise expensive to correct. It could be a faucet that does not work or insufficient electrical wiring so the dishwasher and the microwave cannot run at the same time without throwing a fuse, or a broken stair on the steps to the basement that should be stepped over or stepped on carefully. Everyone in the group knows to avoid it or go around. New people have to be told, but since this avoidance is so ingrained it can be difficult for the group to remember that it should be included in any orientation. An organizational missing stair could be a written policy that everyone ignores or a way of placing book orders that seems cumbersome, but works around an even more cumbersome official process. People can be a missing stair. Something they do is unorthodox or unusual and everyone has just learned to live with it instead of trying to change it early on. Perhaps the person is prone to outbursts or two staff members have an inappropriate personal relationship or someone never comes to meetings, but then will negate decisions made there. As a newcomer you will probably not have the ability to confront a missing stair, but it is important to know who and what they are. In some organizational cultures new people are encouraged to speak up with their opinions and suggestions immediately; in others they are encouraged to learn the organization for a semester or so before doing so. In part it depends on the organization and in part it depends on the individual. Duke and Boyd point out other areas of organizational culture:

> *Informal structures to watch out for as you get settled in and familiar with your new workplace include "rituals" (Is there someone who always starts a meeting?), "myths and legends" (stories about the past that help shape present thinking), "behavioral codes" (Is it okay to be late? What is the dress code? Is joking around in a meeting acceptable?), "shared jargon" (catch phrases), and "prescriptions and preferences" (Is there a "best way" or "expected" way for things to be done?).*
>
> Duke and Boyd (2006, p. 37).

This is an area where an effective mentor can be very useful. At a minimum try to sound out a few people on cultural norms and institutional history. In its simplest form the organizational culture is knowing if people bring in cake on birthdays. In a more complex form it is knowing that while the tenure documents only generally call for scholarship, two peer reviewed articles are needed and one should be single authored.

Reading business advice books can lead to insights not always provided in Academia. One such example is that being right really does not matter. While on the surface this seems contradictory—after all, how can being right not be important? But, often it is not. Many people who are right cannot articulate their ideas effectively to others so the "rightness" does not matter. Some people are so obnoxious that others would rather be wrong than be in the same room with the person who is right. Sometimes the rightness of something takes time to sink in. Nicholas C. Zakas, a software engineer, summed it up this way:

> *At the end of the day, there is very little value to being right. You don't acquire rightness points and just how frequently you are right doesn't end up on your resume. What actually matters are the relationships you have. You can only go as far as the people who want to communicate with you. Being right actually hurts if it interferes with your ability to interact with people. As my former manager said, you should definitely know what is important to you and be willing to fight for it. But let go of the pedantic points you are trying to make—those just don't matter.*
>
> Zakas (2012).

The same point is made in the book *The 'It' Factor* by Mark Wiskup:

> *Being right does not matter. Do not ever expect others to listen to or follow your instructions just because you are right. Being right would not won't do you any good, unless you first make the effort of helping them care about why you are talking to them (Wiskup, 2007, p. 35).*

Rightness is sometimes a relative value. Two ideas are presented at a meeting, each proponent convinced theirs is the right idea. Only one can be used at a time. If the first idea does not pan out the proponent of the second idea can then step forward, but this process will be smoother if everyone had been cordial during the initial discussions. There are also ideas that are articulated before their time. They might have been right, but not everyone was ready to hear it. Clinging to a sense of rightness is as ineffective and damaging as holding a grudge. It interferes with moving forward and takes up mental real estate that can be put to better use.

You might be the smartest, fastest, most efficient, and productive person in the room, but pointing out how slow, inefficient, or unproductive anyone else is will not make friends or influence people. No one runs on all cylinders all the time. Some people's work flow may take a few unnecessary turns; telling them how they can improve (or, worse, telling them you think they are doing it wrong) may not be the best tactic an untenured person can take. A tenured person with a long history of this behavior may find themselves moved to an office in the basement with a leak in the ceiling, or retired sooner than they intended. A person's way of doing things is, to some degree, a function of where he or she is in the technological timeline. A habit once learned is difficult to unlearn, even if newer, better techniques have been developed. As long as it does not impact your workflow it might be a good idea to just let things be. Of course, if advice is asked then offering it, in nonjudgmental terms, is okay. There are ways of wording it, such as "I've heard that it is easier if you ...." or "Someone I used to work with did it this way..." or "I just read ..." or "you've taught me so much I'd like to share something I've just learned." The phrase, or simply an attitude of "I'm right and know more than you" is generally not well received, especially from a junior colleague. Be gracious with your rightness. People are more willing to take advice or admit to a weakness or ignorance of a certain point or procedure if the person they are learning from does not brag about it in public meetings or remind them of it on a regular basis.

Along these same lines, a great deal of boorish behavior is cloaked in the concept of speaking truth to power. It does take courage to speak up and voice your convictions or to point out behavior that you think may be illegal or immoral or to defend someone you think is being unjustly treated, but all of these things can be done in a civil manner, without peacocking or grandstanding. Nor does speaking truth to power always have to be negative. If one is willing to say to power (however that may be defined) "this is wrong and we should not do it" should not that person also be willing to say "this is right and I am glad we are doing it" or "what you did was difficult and it took real leadership to accomplish it"?

Knowing what you want in the larger scheme of things is important, but so is knowing what you want in the smaller matters. When approaching a colleague ask yourself if you just want to vent or if you want advice, are you telling her about a project because you want help planning it out or you are hoping she will help you actually do it. Telling someone at the start that you are not looking for solutions, but just want to blow off steam saves frustration on your part if she starts trying to solve what she perceives as a problem, and saves you the frustration of having to deflect suggestions you did not want. Be upfront if you want advice, but understand the other person may want time to think about it.

Khalil Gibran is quoted as saying "You are the bows from which the living arrows of your children are sent forth." The concept of being a bow or an arrow is equally applicable to a work setting. Some days a person is an arrow, flying forward to new ventures, aiming toward a goal or target. Some days that same person might be a bow, hoisting aloft a colleague or student. The nurturing of new talent (or supporting existing or managerial talent) is always a win win situation. There is no real downside to encouraging others. In times of economic upheaval tapping former protégés can be as profitable as tapping former mentors. John Singleton was an intern and production assistant on Pee-wee Herman's television show when he met actor Laurence Fishburne and musician Ice Cube. He approached both about a movie he wanted to do and have them be involved in. They could have dismissed him but they did not; both encouraged him. A few years later the movie, *Boyz N the Hood*, made all the three very famous and a lot of money (Matloff, 2011). Bill Neukom became Microsoft's first general counsel when, as a young lawyer he was asked by a senior colleague, Bill Gates, Sr., to help Gates's son with a legal matter for his small computer startup. Neukom stayed with Microsoft for almost 25 years, all because he was willing to do a favor for a co-worker's son (Harem, Garland, France, & Cortese, 1998). While most people in academe will not be involved in anything as dramatic, the courtesy and attention paid to younger colleagues and students is seldom wasted, and it can be a bulwark against future adversity. At some future point those talented young protégés might take you off the unemployment line or open the door to a fantastic new opportunity. They are less likely to push out you the door to retirement or resent your (hopefully) larger salary if you have been or continue to be useful to them personally.

The reverse of that is working with a mentor. Some institutions have a formal mentoring program. This can run the gamut from "onboarding 101" to co-authoring a peer-reviewed journal article together. Peterson notes that librarians might have more than one mentor:

> As an academic librarian, you may want to pursue a mentoring relationship with more than one person to aid you in developing different skills. For example, you could work with one colleague whose instructional skills are excellent in order to improve your teaching, and another who is adept at management to develop your supervisory skills. You may also form a series of bonds over the years, learning from different people as their expertise and support become relevant to you at different times.
>
> Peterson (2005, p. 84).

Informal mentoring might occur naturally or the newer librarian can contact the more senior librarian directly. In general this is a quest based on either proximity or a specific skill set. For example, "I really admire your ability to run conferences. Could I help you with the next one?" A librarian new to publishing might approach a librarian with experience in that area and ask for advice, either generally or on a specific aspect of publishing. Granted, the person with those skills may like being the only person around with them, so a more subtle approach may be required. One tactic Sheryl Sandberg points out in *Lean In* is to offer something in return. In librarianship, a knowledge of statistics for a research project or the ability to create artful nametags for a conference or to simply be a proofreader are ways to be useful. Often people are interested in free labor, provided the person offering it does not become more trouble than she is worth. Sandberg writes:

> Studies show that mentors select protégés based on performance and potential. Intuitively, people invest in those who stand out for their talent or who can really benefit from help. Mentors continue to invest when mentees use their time well and are truly open to feedback. It may turn into a friendship, but the foundation is a professional relationship. Given this, I believe we have sent the wrong message to young women. We need to stop telling them, "Get a mentor and you will excel." Instead, we need to tell them, "Excel and you will get a mentor."
>
> Sandberg (2013, p. 68).

She sums up her view by saying "I realized that searching for a mentor has become the professional equivalent of waiting for Prince Charming" (Sandberg, 2013, p. 66).

People are different with different needs, skills and ways of doing things. Respecting other people's boundaries (or lack thereof), especially when they are different from your own, learning to be grateful for the work they do and ways they enhance your own efforts (even if that was not their intent), and appreciating their dedication to the organization are better than focusing on negatives. Taking the time to try and understand another person's view and why they may act or react as they do instead of reacting negatively to their actions or words makes for a more productive workplace and a lot less office stress. These are not always easy things to do and they may take some effort and may not be reciprocated, but if looking forward and being productive are goals then these are necessities.

Working well with people is an asset, and one that is often undervalued. Like time management, it is an integral strategy for any career path. Developing good working relationships is an asset, and like all assets, worthy of noting.

Librarianship

4

This is the "bread and butter" chapter. For librarians of any stripe, any type of library, any level of status (tenure, non-tenure, public, academic, and so on) this is the day-to-day activity that makes up the bulk of our jobs. In a tenure-track job this aspect of work can get short shrift, lost in the pressure to publish, or be involved in professional associations. Yet, it is the day-to-day work that matters most. A stellar publication record will not compensate for poor annual reviews or the lack of support from colleagues. Effective day-to-day work can, however, provide the inspirations for research and the impetus for contacting our colleagues at other institutions, as well as campus letters for tenure or promotion packets. For example, you need to be a part of a technical services library group because you have questions about your daily work, or because you need communicate with others who use the same vendor products, or if a public services librarian, to reach out for help answering a patron's question.

David Foster Wallace gave a commencement speech at Kenyon University in 2005, later published in book form in 2009 that started out with a story of two young fish encountering an older fish who asks them "How's the water?" One of the younger fish looks at the other and asks "What's water?" That is often how daily activities are viewed. They surround us and are so much a part of us so that we do not even notice them. As water is with fish, so librarianship is with librarians. Wallace goes on to talk about the mundane aspects of life that can weigh us down, grocery shopping, bill paying, commuting back and forth to work. Yet, it is in these daily activities that we can have the most impact, whether it is to say a kind word or simply view things in a more positive light, and they can be a way of connecting us to the rest of the world. It is the day-to-day activities that sustain us—the acquisition and preparation of food, health checkups, bill paying, and so on; if we stopped doing those things we would quickly lose our homes and starve.

Likewise, academic librarians cannot forget, in the rush and relative glamor of publishing and presenting, of meetings with deans and higher ranking campus officials, that hundreds or thousands of 18-year olds find themselves washed up on our shores every September. The library is a daunting place to them. They need to learn to use it, the items they find therein (physically or digitally) should be easy to locate and relevant, the staff should be friendly and helpful. Graduate students are anxious for research opportunities, and need library materials as primary sources, or at least to find supporting documentation for literature reviews. Classroom and research faculty are doing their own research and need support for that and their classroom activities. Staff are also involved in research or need information for other work related or personal reasons. All of these people should feel that the library and the librarians are there for them.

4.1 Within the library

Each librarian has specific duties related to their job that fit within the larger organization. Hopefully these are spelled out in the job description, but there may be other duties attached that were not included. As people settle into their daily activities they may absorb or lose certain responsibilities depending on personality, interest, and current institutional need. Over time jobs duties will shift as well. However, at any given time, it is imperative, and this cannot be said often or forcefully enough, that each librarian be able to articulate verbally and in writing, what it is they do and how that fits into the larger organization. In the business world this is sometimes referred to as an "elevator speech." If you find yourself in the elevator with the organization president or a high-level official or some other gatekeeper and they ask you what you do, what would you tell them? An elevator ride is always short, so the elevator speech is, by necessity, only a minute or so long. Assume the person does not understand the intricacies of librarianship, or of that particular corner of it. A cataloger might say to another librarian, "I catalog serials." That is easy enough to understand, at least for another librarian, but how to quickly describe cataloging to a non-librarian? One might say "I decide what call number the books will have" or "I make sure books and journals are assigned to a place on the shelves where people would be most likely to find them." A reference or instruction librarian might say "I help students find the best resources for their assignments, to make sure they write thoughtful papers."

This is another place where understanding how the tenure process works comes in handy. At any institution where a tenure packet goes outside the library for final approval, it will be read by people who may have little or no understanding of how the library works. An "elevator speech" description of what you do should be a part of the tenure narrative. Slaughter writes about this in Miller, McDonald, and Jia (2005):

> If you have promoted your achievements throughout the years, the librarians on your tenure committee will have a reasonable understanding of your duties as a serialist, but most nonlibrarian members of the tenure review process will not have a clue unless you tell them in your dossier (48).

Librarians' tenure documents are sometimes the only way administrators and senior faculty learn about what librarians do. It is your obligation to help them understand what it is the university is funding when money goes into the library budget.

Each job specialty will have its own rewards and pitfalls. Public service librarians have to maintain a balance between helping people find resources and doing it for them. This balance will differ with various populations. A dean who asks you to find a few recent articles on a topic is different from a student who has an assignment to find a few recent articles on a topic and asks you to do it for them. Occasionally a student becomes a problem by consistently wanting a lot of a librarian's time, whether to go over an assignment in great detail or ask the same questions repeatedly or wish to talk about details of their personal life. A librarian who does students' work for them is not really doing them any favors, nor is having a regular chat session with a student for an hour or so every week doing the librarian any favors as at least some of that time

or extended email discussions. One of the French faculty received a grant to purchase French-Canadian literature and I shepherded the orders through the library's acquisition system. I also used standard reviewing tools to order books for the collection generally. In keeping with the university's new strategic plan and a renewed emphasis on student retention I worked with the Office of Student Affairs to develop programs and events designed to foster a sense of connection with the campus. One of these was a mystery night event in the library just before finals. I also participated in the library's outreach program to area high schools, which included a Minecraft-themed tour of the library.

In each scenario, which of the two librarians would be most likely to get a merit raise or tenure? Beth and Patrice probably sat down to do their annual report and wondered what they had done the previous year. Cassandra and Sam had to do a little more work keeping track of what they did, but it is worth the effort to paint a more detailed picture of how they contributed to the library and the campus. Anyone reading it will have a better idea of how their job interacts with the library and university at large. They could have gone into more detail about the specifics of what they do on a daily basis—was it copy cataloging or original cataloging? How many people came to mystery night? For a brief annual report these paragraphs would be sufficient, but for a longer tenure document there would need to be a great deal more detail. Their statements also provide the director with information for the library's annual report. If their statements go outside the library it provides a clear picture of how their department work and interact with other areas in the library for the benefit of the entire institution. Beth's and Patrice's statements provide none of this. Likewise, it is possible that Beth and Patrice did as much or more than Cassandra and Sam, but we will never know since they did not include the details of their work.

As mentioned in the previous chapter, it is customary for tenure and promotion, as well as merit raise, committees to only be able to consider what is in front of them. You know your work better than anyone and should be your own best advocate. In all cases highlighting individual accomplishments is important, but most libraries are collaborative organizations and so mentioning work done with others presents the entire unit in a positive light.

Even within departments or among people doing similar jobs there is a tendency to either assume everyone knows what we do, or on the opposite extreme to keep that as quiet as possible to avoid interference. For people whose job duties take them out of their colleagues' sphere it is vital that they keep everyone up to date on what they are doing. A librarian who does not seem to be around much may be taking on a lot of evening chat reference shifts or active in library outreach to campus dormitories or very involved offsite in working with a new technology. What the other librarians see, though, is that the person is not there. Out of sight, out of mind. When the annual review comes around, they might send in feedback that implies the person is shirking their duties or just that the department does not have a good feel for what they are doing. You do not want your colleagues to develop the idea that you are not doing anything. This is especially true for librarians whose regular duties take place at a time or location when others are not around. Graduate students, new librarians, and staff might take jobs working in the evening or on weekends, when most of the other people in the library are not there. They never or seldom see you. Suppose a full-time position comes open. If you apply for the job will the search committee have any sense of who you are other than perhaps a name on group memos or emails? Will they have any idea what you have accomplished? Indeed, do you have any set tasks other than staff a desk? If you apply for another job what kind of reference can you expect? In the best scenario the people at the library where you work will be looking for ways to keep you on or if that is not possible, are mentioning your name to friends in other departments or schools as a good potential hire. They would be forwarding you job ads and suggesting places you might look for work. To do that they have to know you, what you are doing, what your job interests are, and what your career plan is.

If departmental meetings have an agenda item for people to talk about what they are working on, by all means speak up. If you do not have that public opportunity, send around an email telling everyone that you have not disappeared, but that you are working hard elsewhere, and give some specifics. For those whose job is during off hours, send the occasional email, commenting on a new policy or mentioning a situation you have seen developing and providing suggestions on how to deal with it. Night and weekend workers can sometimes spot issues that will become problems during the week; let people know about them. Ask if you can help out on any particular projects or just offer your assistance generally, with your immediate supervisor's permission, of course. If the department has adopted new software, volunteer to write up some tips for using it or provide some feedback on what you have learned while using it. Offer to give an update or a demonstration of what you are doing at a departmental meeting or a system-wide library meeting.

Spelling out in some detail what one's work involves allows the library as a whole to better understand what goes on, and allows the university at large to see how its money is being spent. It provides opportunities for more and better public relations. Library directors, by and large, like to have talking points and bragging rights. They also do not like being blind-sided, so finding out what a librarian has been doing from someone else on campus is generally not a good thing from the director's point of view. Of course there are always exceptions, and at very large institutions librarians are more apt to report to a division or department head. Regardless of the reporting structure, individuals need to let administration (and their colleagues) know what they are doing, most especially at annual report time, but also at appropriate times during the year. It would be very frustrating for one librarian to take the time and energy to write a grant application for a project only to discover than another librarian has already started on something similar with internal funding. There is a balance between wanting to let the powers that be know what the library is doing and avoiding unwanted interference from forces outside (and sometimes within) the library; senior librarians and administrators can help find that balance.

Any one librarian who develops quicker, shorter, or more efficient way of doing something should offer to share it with others. Hopefully within departmental meetings there is time for a quick "round robin" so that each person has a minute or two to mention anything they have been working on (another "elevator speech" opportunity). Here is a time to broach the idea of new software products that might help everyone do their job better, or news gleaned from committee meetings, or notes about new issues or problems that might affect others. The last thing you want is for everyone to find out you created a shortcut that would have saved them time and you did not share it. Interdepartmental projects or initiatives are a byproduct of talking about current projects or projects that might be interesting to do in the future. When digitization staff talk to the grants office they can find areas of common interest, and possible projects that might be grant worthy. When special collections librarians talk with bibliographers they can build upon existing strengths to create truly exceptional library collections. If the library's reserves policy or procedures changes not only does the reserve staff need to know, but public services librarians and circulation staff do as well, to make sure they are giving out correct information. A casual conversation reveals that two librarians have both been drafting proposals to be part of a campus-wide initiative. One might bow out this year to prepare a more detailed proposal next year, or they might join forces to create a stronger proposal; in any event, they will both know there is at least one other library proposal being submitted. While no one is an island we remain unconnected archipelagos unless each of us knows what the others are doing.

If the job you are in is likely to be a stepping stone to a job you want, or if you have career ambitions, in a healthy workplace it is acceptable to talk about them from time to time. In a collegial atmosphere people generally want to help other people. This is not to say that your goals would come before the institutional or departmental goals, but if people know that you would like to increase your project management skills they might let you know when an opportunity in that area will become available. Look for tasks that need to be done or will enhance the department without creating extra work for others. Librarians with a specific interest in social media could offer to open an account for the library on a platform, provided that is not encroaching on someone's turf.

Territoriality can come into play in group settings, and part of understanding organizational culture is to recognize what the informal boundaries might be. A new librarian hired to primarily do freshman instruction might inadvertently cause a rift by approaching faculty in a subject area and offering to do instruction for them when there is a subject bibliographer who has been cultivating that same department. In a perfect world any instruction done for the department would be a plus, but in the real world encroaching on another librarian's designated area can be fraught with difficulty. In a situation where the new hire has a graduate degree in that subject area it would be understandable for her to have an interest in the field, but the situation should be approached with some delicacy. For example, the new hire might offer to refresh some existing guides that have become a bit stale, or when talking with faculty offer to put them in touch with the designated bibliographer. You do not want to give colleagues the impression that you are more interested in someone else's job than in your own. Unless your daily work is completely caught up and done well it is not a good idea to step uninvited into someone else's. You also want to avoid being pulled into someone else's job so completely that you own will suffer.

In the hiring process there should be some mention of professional development money. These are funds that can be used for conferences or training programs. In an academic setting there is also usually some form of tuition remission available. I took ample use of these benefits. After getting an undergraduate degree I found a staff position in the university library (having worked there as a student) and took classes toward a masters in library science. As a full-time employee I only had to pay one-fourth of the tuition. At one or two classes a semester it took several years to earn my degree, and graduate school was more or less my hobby. With an MLS and staff experience in two departments I was able to get a professional library job and then use tuition benefits at that school to earn a second master's degree, again taking one or two classes a semester. A number of other librarians have followed similar career paths. Some go on to earn additional graduate degrees. Other take advantage of certificate programs that are available in the area or online. The Medical Library Association offers a special accreditation program resulting in membership in the Academy of Health Information Professionals. If the degrees or programs are job related in any way your employer might pay the fee, provided it is reasonable.

Someone whose evenings and weekends are free of extensive family obligations would have time for any number of educational and career building activities, as well as a modest social life. Those with family obligations will have a tougher time, but if the classes or assignments can be considered job related in any way it might be possible to combine them with work responsibilities and do them on the job. Think of how your class or program would benefit the library or institution as a whole and approach your department head or director about working out a schedule for it and what immediate projects you might use in your class assignments. Do keep in mind that if your employer invests in your education they will expect a return and you may be tagged as the in-house expert in this area, even if your personal interests go in a different direction.

Most institutions will have some form of annual review, with a more involved review process at promotion, tenure, or when a continuing contract is up for renewal. As those points are coming closer read over the guidelines again to make sure you know who will be evaluating you and when. In a shared governance or tenure setting everyone in the department or unit may be able to submit comments, with a smaller group writing up an official document. That usually goes to a department head or director for another level of review and another formal document. In larger organizations the packet goes to another level, for review by a system-wide committee. In a tenure setting there is usually a university-wide committee after that, which reviews all tenure packets from all departments and schools. Make sure you understand the process and in what format you should submit your materials. This is opportunity, perhaps the only opportunity, for you to tell your story to the university at large, who you are, what your job is, and why it is important to the school. To do that, you have to understand all of those things. Regardless of what you publish or what offices you hold, it is the day-to-day aspect of librarianship that ties it all together.

4.2 Within the institution

The library is the heart of the university! This is said frequently. The corollary being that, like the heart, no one pays any attention to it until it is failing. It is unseen, but it pumps material throughout the larger body. Likewise the library makes information available to everyone connected to the university, onsite or online, but the inner workings are hidden. Journal costs, digitization processes, book selection, cataloging, teaching freshmen how to find articles, all of these things are generally invisible. Departmental liaison librarians do touch base with teaching faculty, and other librarians interact with the larger institution through committees, working groups, and individual contacts, but, by and large, the work of the university goes on without interacting with the library or librarians on a regular basis.

One way to make sure that the library is recognized is to be part of the game. To be part of the game you have to be on the field. It is said that if you are not at the table you are on the menu. What all of this means is that you need to be active and involved. So librarians, especially those with faculty status, need to take part in faculty affairs. This means sitting on committees that can seem very boring and unproductive. Sometimes simply being in the room is the productivity. The library being represented, acknowledged, part of the process, equal to the other participants makes it valuable in reminding the others that the library exists and that librarians are present and part of the group. If librarians are faculty there should be a librarian on the faculty governing bodies and that person should attend meetings. I have been the library's representative on the Arts & Science Faculty Senate for a number of years, voicing comments occasionally but primarily simply being present. And at one of those meetings someone proposed amendments to the senate bylaws to tie up a few loose ends and clean up some confusing language. Along the way there was a sentence included that a librarian could attend but would not have voting rights. Had a librarian not been in the room to ask if that sentence could be removed (it was), the library would have lost its voice on that body. Words on paper matter and if the library is not included it will all too easily be forgotten. Having a librarian on the curriculum committee offers the opportunity to broach information literacy as a formal part of the curriculum. Sometimes simply being in the room reminds people that the library exists and someone else will bring up library-related issues. Most institutional committee work falls more under the service category than the librarianship category, but others are more pertinent to the day-to-day activities of a librarian. When preparing your packet if you are not sure what category something should be in, ask a more senior colleague.

Libraries are not likely to be included in campus digital projects unless librarians are present when the process is designed. Faculty contracts designed or negotiated without the input of a librarian leads to problems such as family leave policies based on release from classroom teaching, which is not directly relatable to librarians' jobs. Strong faculty and staff connections can create a more inclusionary process—someone asking "how will this affect the library?" or "shouldn't we have a librarian involved?" but, as a safeguard, having a librarian in the room when the process is designed is a good idea.

Librarians need to attend campus activities, as noted in a previous chapter. People may not seek out a librarian to ask a question, but if someone stumbles across one at a reception or a concert or a strategic planning meeting, they might ask the question then, as their memory is jogged by the sight of a librarian. While librarians, like other academics, can tend toward introversion, it is vitally important to see and be seen. Sometimes this is as simple as using the faculty locker room at the campus gym, or eating in the college cafeteria. If librarians are never spotted on campus they become like Keebler elves or Willy Wonka's oompa loompas, rumored to exist but never really seen. This is not good for anyone. Set a benchmark, for example, to attend at least one campus or institutional event every month that school is in session. This would need to be adjusted based on the size of the institution, more opportunities are available at larger institutions, people at smaller institutions may need to set a different goal, such as attend at least one event a semester and eat in the campus cafeteria at least once a month.

One common mistake at events is for people from one department to go as a group and talk primarily among themselves. It is one thing if this group does not see each other on a daily basis and the intra-group networking opportunity is unusual, it is another if this is a group that regular meets either formally or informally. Generally speaking, at meetings or a larger body, one might arrive and or leave with a departmental colleague, but they should separate soon after entering and spend the time there talking with people they do not see regularly. Marc Kramer, in his book *Power Networking*, lists ten keys to being a great networking. Two are "never sit with colleagues from your own company at an event," and "never sit with a friend you normally socialize with at an event" (Kramer, 1988, p. 3). As he says, this would not widen your network.

With pressing deadlines and the necessity to publish hovering overhead taking the time to attend receptions may seem frivolous, but consider it a part of your job, because it is. Being a part of the faculty means being part of the larger faculty unit—the university. If no one ever saw any of the math professors there would be some talk about what it is exactly that they do and why are they so stand offish or stuck up. Declining to be included in any of the social aspects of campus effectively removes you from the faculty unit. Granted not everyone will want to attend all events, but there should be more than the same one or two librarians attending.

For departmental liaisons being seen is especially important. Newly hired librarians need to make themselves known to classroom faculty in their areas. Sending a group email or a printed introductory letter is the bare basic minimum. Librarians must find out where the faculty offices are, where the classroom faculty might be while on campus, and go there once in a while. Note office hours and stop by for an in-person introduction. Trying to set up an in-person meeting can be tricky as schedules change, but office hours are generally kept. It might take a few tries since students will also be trying to talk with their professor, but going over a couple of times will surely result in one visit when the professor has a few spare moments. Finding out that person's individual research interests is also important. These are usually listed on campus, departmental, or personal websites. As new books come in or as you come across articles in that field, write a brief note and with the photocopied book cover and table of contents or a send an email with an attached copy of the article or a link to the full text; this will remind the researcher that you exist and can be helpful. Librarians who do not directly work with classroom faculty will say it is equally important for them to be seen on campus, simply as a reminder that they exist, and provide an opportunity to mention what it is they do.

That being said it could be just as or more important for non-liaison librarians to attend campus social events. Unlike liaison librarians they do not have built in connections to one or more departments. They will have to forge those connections on their own. Campus letters of support for non-liaison librarians can be a challenge. A librarian who works with social media or exclusively with freshmen or in more technical aspects of the library will have to make a particular effort to build enough goodwill for someone to write a letter for them. Campus events and receptions are a good place to do that. A digitization librarian might run into one of the aforementioned hypothetical seldom-seen math professors who is trying to digitize some old papers or an art history professor who wants to create online copies of slides she uses regularly for a class. A social media librarian might find out that the dean is interested in setting up a WordPress blog and her assistant will need some help with it. You might find out someone is trying to set up a departmental library of old science (or math) textbooks for students to use for practice. You might be withdrawing just such books from the library shelves and can offer to give them to the department. Hopefully library colleagues will help new hires meet people with whom they have common interests, but they may not fully understand what those interests are. Working a room at a campus social event is difficult for most people, but it is a great way to find people to work with on projects or ways to make sure the library remains relevant to the university.

This might be the appropriate place to mention a piece of advice a very cultured and more experienced librarian once gave me. Always keep a box of blank cards in your office. This might be replaced by personalized departmental stationary, but there are also occasions where a card with an artistic scene on the front is a better choice. In modern times sending an article as an email attachment is possible, perhaps preferably, but sometimes a hand-written note is more personal. Attaching a "thinking of you" or "thought you might enjoy this" note to a photocopy is a clear demonstration that you have learned and remembered what someone's interests are and have taken the time to alert them to a relevant item. It demonstrates an ability to locate relevant information and is likely to lead to official requests for assistance with projects or referrals for students to contact you. Take note of campus newsletters and see who is mentioned, either because they were tenured or promoted, published a book, got a grant, or any number of other announcements. This might be a good time to send a congratulations note. Emails work well for many of these, but on special occasions a personal note in the mail can make a bigger impression. You will always have a closer relationship with some faculty and staff than others, just by nature of personal friendships, and will keep in closer touch with those people, but notes to a wider range of faculty or staff now and then can help maintain ties between those departments and the library.

Many institutions which consider librarians faculty will require letters of support from peers on campus, or at least some sign of interaction. Tenure packets certainly will require such documentation. The previous chapter suggested talking with tenured librarians to find out what their packets looked like, reviewing guidelines and process documents, and, in general, finding out as much as possible what a successful tenure packet looked like and contained. This is definitely an aspect of the tenure packet that should be discussed, to see what is required and what the current cultural expectation is. If only a certain number of letters are required then it is easy enough to approach those individuals with whom the librarian has had the most positive interaction. Anyone on campus should have a good idea how to structure such a letter.

However, in a request it is acceptable to mention how one has interacted with that individual. For example, a public services librarian might say "I've spoken to several of your classes, including [name class] which included an in-depth research project, and met with a number of your students to help them individually. We also served on [name of campus committee] together." This will jog the person's memory and perhaps add some details to the letter. Savvy letter writers might ask "is there anything in particular you would like me to mention?" This is not a time to be coy. If there is something you would specifically like the letter writer to address, mention it. This tactic also applies to job references. When asking if someone would be a job reference it is acceptable to say "you are the person I've worked most closely with on instruction so if you could mention that I would appreciate it." This alerts the reference to the fact that other references would not be able to speak to the job candidate's experience in that area with as much detail.

It is also useful to have some documentation to show that others have been pleased with the librarian's work. People may not always recognize that such documentation is useful. Therefore, after a classroom presentation or at the end of an involved project, or when a committee project, or one's term on a committee is over, a strategy might be to send the professor or committee chair an email saying you enjoyed working with the class or on the project. Such a message will very possibly elicit a response, acknowledging the work done. A few of the more effusive or lengthy emails can be added to a packet to demonstrate one's worth. Even in a non-tenure situation, it is useful to keep a few emails or notes of this kind every year and store them in an "attaboy/ attagirl" file. An earlier chapter mentioned the utility of printing and keeping some emails that acknowledge work or comment on the librarian's involvement in projects. This is where those emails come in handy. In the chapter on counting assets, I mentioned that I tally up what I have done at the end of each month. I staple or otherwise attach any useful or complimentary emails I have received that month to that month's report. At the end of the year I can look through the attachments and select a group that, considered together, present me in a good light. Like an Impressionist painting they will be small dots alone, but put together they make a beautiful picture.

Among the many terrors that can visit a librarian preparing a reappointment or tenure packet is the realization that he or she has formed no connections on campus, never been to an event, never served on a campus-wide committee, never spoken to anyone outside the library, or cannot name a simple person on campus who could or would be willing to write a letter on his or her behalf. This is an endeavor that takes some time, connections have to be developed, reputations built, and so on. If a particular job does not involve consistent or even occasional interaction with the larger organization then the person in that job will need to actively find ways to create that interaction. This could mean volunteering to serve on campus committees, or to seek out faculty or staff on campus whose jobs are in some way related to theirs. For some people this would be one of the more difficult aspects of putting together a packet, if letters of this kind are required or expected. If it seems a particularly daunting task, it might be feasible to ask around and see if there are any acceptable substitutions.

Tracking data can also be helpful in deciding how to approach different departments. I tracked interactions with students and classroom faculty from a number of liaison departments over a period of years and discovered that classroom faculty in one department tended to seek me out themselves and the classroom faculty in another tended to send their students to me. Knowing this made contacting new hires easier, as the approach could be more specifically tailored to what the departmental culture was. This did not require extensive use of statistical math or a spreadsheet, merely notations in my calendar that a question had come in from a professor or a student in a particular department, summarized in monthly reports, and then on annual reports. Comparing a few years' worth of data showed a significant difference in disciplines.

And, of course, keeping in touch with the departmental secretary or administrative assistant can be very useful. The stereotype of the all-powerful departmental secretary is very often based in fact. This is the person who can get you a list of adjunct faculty teaching that semester or tell you how many students are in a given class. She can also remind the classroom faculty that you are there and could be helpful or useful with particular situations. Creating a connection with staff, more so than creating connections with faculty, requires getting out of the library. Staff are less likely to be in your space so you must go to theirs. When taking a new job, or switching liaison departments, or when there is staff turnover, make a point to send over a welcome note to departmental support staff and follow-up with an in-person visit. The emphasis in these conversations should not be on what that person can do for you, but what you can do for that person: help tracking down information for departmental faculty and finding materials they themselves might need. As many of our mothers told us when we were young, it always pays to be nice to people who are frequently overlooked. As a mother myself I found that courteous and respectful behavior toward school secretaries and facilities staff is not only a virtue unto itself, but always provided benefits geometrically greater than the time invested. The same goes for academic staff, such as administrative assistants.

Library faculty and staff who work with technology can benefit from meeting their peers across campus; for example, hosting or setting up an "ITea" or lunch meeting. These need not be overly formal and are often a good excuse to meet up for conversation, venting, sharing, and brainstorming. It can also ease the loneliness factor when few people have similar responsibilities in any given unit. Here again are opportunities to network, help each other out, and possibly develop the ties needed for peer letters when it is time to prepare a packet.

It also must be said that there are frequent opportunities to step up and become an in-house expert on something. New technologies pop up faster than any one individual can track. A library may be very well versed in RefWorks as a bibliographic software, but when new faculty start asking about Zotero there needs to be someone who can answer those questions. In some organizations someone might be assigned to learn it, but often it is an organic development—one or more people have some familiarity with it or start to learn. They become the "go to" people for Zotero. Likewise new databases, new techniques, new open source products, all appear on the horizon. Social media platforms are another avenue; new platforms are coming out all the time and a "go to" person can be very helpful. New programs start, new offices open on campus. Someone needs to greet the newcomers, find out who they are, what they are doing, what library materials they might need. This might be a director-level activity;

it might be something that would logically fall to someone else in the system. On the other hand it might not, and an opportunity to chat up the new staffers at a campus reception or in the cafeteria or another local event would be a chance to find out what has already been done, and to refer them to the proper person, or to develop a new role for yourself, if it is something that appeals to you.

4.3   Finding allies

Everyone needs a support group or people to whom they can appeal in case of problems. I have a list of neighbors and their phone numbers stuck to the refrigerator door. This was especially comforting when I was expecting my second child. My husband and I did not have family in the area and were worried about what would happen if I went into labor in the night—who would care for our older child, a preschooler? We live on a friendly street and some of the neighbors said they could be called, any time, and would come over and stay with the older child until my husband could come home from the hospital. As it turned out we did not need to call upon them, but it eased our minds considerably to know that we could. In the workplace, there is a similar need for such contacts. Who to call if an office computer fails? What to do if a vendor question comes up? There are usually set procedures for such eventualities, but going through a phone tree is not as comforting as knowing you have someone's individual number or email. You will need sources to tap for informal information. A liaison librarian needs to know if positions are open in those departments and whether or not they will be filled. That would be important for collection development purposes if nothing else. Forging these connections is most often done through networking, the aforementioned committees, receptions, and so on. The clichéd gift of baked goods does not hurt either.

When several untenured librarians are hired within a few years they have a ready-made writing and/or support group. Unless there are personality issues involved they should get together a few times a year if not monthly to talk about their progress toward tenure, their research projects, things they have found helpful or not, and so on. Some institutions have a formal mentor program; if available this should be taken advantage of. Simply the act of meeting with a mentor, even if the two never become close friends, can be very helpful. At the very least this is someone who can provide some guidance on institutional culture and how to avoid pitfalls at that particular workplace. If librarians there have tenure a mentor should be able to provide guidance on that as well. Even if there is not a formal mentoring program a new hire should try to find an informal mentor, perhaps more than one. It is always a good idea to sound out as many people as possible on an issue before making a decision.

The thought process in the chapter on deciding what you want is helpful here—knowing what you want helps you decide who can help you get there, and thus what sort of allies you need. It is important to make sure you approach potential allies in such a way that they view the alliance as equally valuable to both parties. Otherwise you are asking someone to volunteer their time on your behalf.

4.4   Monotonous excellence

Manufacturers and small investors aim for monotonous excellence, doing the same thing over and over and not making errors. This should also be the aim for the librarianship aspect of a librarian's job. Day-to-day interactions with classroom faculty, colleagues, and students should be handled quickly and competently, if not brilliantly. Granted, this is a standard that is nearly impossible to meet all the time, but it is a goal to aim for.

The main job of a transit system is for the trains to run on time. Regardless of how beautifully the cars are painted, if the trains are not dependable it does not matter. The transit system may sponsor popular community events, but if the trains are unreliable ridership will go down. What matters is that the trains are monotonously excellent— they run on time, day in day out, rain or shine.

This is an area where organizational skills and rote efficiency come in very handy. For liaison librarians a friendship, or at least a positive connection, with a departmental secretary can be helpful in getting copies of syllabi (if they have gone through the departmental secretary—many are done solely through course management systems), to see who might have library-intensive assignments. Sending out notes to new faculty and reminders to others, outlining what the library can do for them. Access services librarians will want to review reserve procedures and have everything ready for new students and faculty, have information available and broadcast it through a variety of channels, stating library services and policies. In summation, librarianship is the core of every librarian's job. You need to know what your job entails, take on additional responsibilities when opportunity arises, especially those that will benefit you, and document what you do.

Scholarship 5

There is nothing as terrifying as a blank sheet of paper or a blinking cursor on an empty screen. For many librarians at tenure-track institutions the research and publication requirements are the most intimidating. The type of research required will vary from institution to institution. As mentioned in previous chapters, it is important to understand the requirements at any individual institution. Looking at recent tenure packets and talking with people who have served on reappointment or tenure committees will provide a good idea what is needed. Librarians who are not at tenure-track institutions, but who think they might like to work at one someday, librarians who will soon be on the job market (including newly minted librarians), and people who just like to write, might find it useful, and a bit challenging, to explore publication and presentation opportunities, even if they are not required to do so. It can be a little tricky to be the only librarian at a library who publishes. Corporate culture will provide some clues on whether or not this activity should be widely broadcast or only sparingly mentioned in the office; on personal or work-related social media, of course, you may broadcast your accomplishments at will. At tenure-track institutions some form of scholarship will be a necessity.

This chapter will be longer than the others in this book as it is an area that librarians may be less familiar with than librarianship or service. All librarians do librarianship and very few can get through even the earliest stages of a career without sitting on a committee. Scholarship, however, is not practiced everywhere or by all librarians; therefore it needs a little more explanation.

Scholarship can usually be defined as published articles, chapters, or books, or conference presentations, though there is a lot of interplay between the two. One builds upon the other. Scholarship might also refer to being involved in the editorial process, editing books, journals, or other publications, though some people place this in the service category. Hopefully the newly hired librarian or academic will have reviewed the tenure requirements and have an idea of the kind of mix needed at that particular institution. Is the single authored peer-reviewed journal article the requirement for tenure? Even if that is the case it is unlikely someone will go up for tenure with just one article. There will be an assortment of presentations and publications. That might be one single authored peer-reviewed journal article, a co-authored peer-reviewed article, an article in a nonpeer-reviewed publication, and a few book reviews, along with one or two conference presentations. Another option might be a co-authored peer-reviewed journal article, editorship of an association newsletter, and a few nonpeer-reviewed articles. This is another reason why talking with the newly tenured or promoted or looking at recent packets can be very useful. What sort of materials did people have, how were they arranged, so on. This will provide some guidelines, if none are formally written, on what is expected. It is vitally important to understand where digital projects, scholarly blog posts, and other online endeavors fall in the scholarship hierarchy.

Different people write differently and, as also mentioned in previous chapters, it is important to understand one's individual style. Some work diligently, a little each day, others tend to procrastinate and then do marathon writing sessions. Some combine both methods, with periods of diligent writing and periods of putting it aside. In the second chapter, the concept of "knowing where you are" was mentioned. This is part of that, knowing or learning the best writing style for you. This can also help when collaborating—knowing your own writing style allows you to adapt it a little (or a lot) to coordinate well with your collaborators. This can avoid a lot of frustration.

The easiest way to avoid the terror of starting from scratch is to never start from scratch. How is that done? For new librarians, start with graduate school papers. Are there any papers written while in graduate school that can be revised, expanded, or built up into an article or a presentation? Are there any project or committee reports written as part of your job that can be expanded into articles? Also mentioned in previous chapters is the importance of interests outside of work. These are also fodder for scholarship. More ideas for never starting from scratch are detailed later in this chapter.

Starting a new job that encourages or requires scholarship, especially a new tenure-track job, means the clock is ticking as soon as work starts on the first day. For some, it starts sooner, if their job begins in August and the tenure clock started ticking in July. In the chaos of learning a new institutional culture and settling into daily job activities the prospect of starting a brand new research project can be daunting, as it should be because that is a very daunting prospect. Scholarship can also be a little lonely as it is often done alone. This can be problematic for some. Writing in *Faculty Career Paths*, Bataille and Brown note "female faculty who feel alienated within a department often spend more time teaching, advising, and mentoring students which 'puts them in contact with others' when they do not feel connected to their colleagues; these activities may, ironically, take them away from activities that are more important to their success" (Bataille & Brown, 2006, p. 71).

One way to combat that is to join or start a writing or research group. If you are one of several new hires in a short time frame then you have a ready-made group. Set up regular meeting times, over lunch or coffee for a more social feel or in a conference room during the regular day for a more official tone. Talk about your projects, what you are thinking about, how your planning is going, where you are in the process. Ask your fellow group members to read drafts or comment on your presentation plans. A writing or research group is also a good place to vent about the stress and pressures of deadlines and job worries. There is a variety of thought on when to start planning a research agenda. Lang suggests that classroom faculty not expect to write anything their first semester (Lang, 2005, p. 50). Parker, writing for law librarians, suggests "hitting the ground running" (Parker, 2011, p. 203). Miller suggests you start planning early (Miller, McDonald, & Jia, 2005, p. 51). Furstenberg says if you are not asking people to review drafts or outlines in your first year you should pick up the pace (Furstenberg, 2013, p. 93). I tend to agree with those who suggest at least planning something earlier rather than later. The scholarship process can take time and the clock is ticking. Spires suggests setting specific deadlines, wanting to complete an article by a certain date (Spires, 2007, p. 105). Furstenberg recommends developing a routine for writing (Furstenberg, 2013, p. 91).

To get something "on the boards" as soon as possible look at what already exists. The aforementioned graduate school papers are an excellent starting point for recent grads or for people who have been taking classes toward another degree. Are any of those papers suitable for presentation or publication with a little work? If not, they may be usable with more effort as time permits. What about work projects at a previous job? Any presentations or poster sessions at a previous job or in graduate school? Can they be expanded into a short article? What aspects of the previous job are different from the current job? Would a brief (or involved) survey of librarians in similar jobs at other institutions provide a snapshot of current best practices or the range of current practices? (For any project involving surveys or test subjects, check with the institution's human subjects review board to see what their rules and regulations are and what permissions might be needed.) If librarianship is a second career is there anything from your previous line of work that could used for scholarship? Book reviews can be a good place to start or short articles in association newsletters. Anything that can be sent out quickly buys time for a longer more involved project. It shows that you are working on something. A tenure or promotion packet with only one or two items on it, and those done or published close to the deadline gives the impression that the librarian did nothing for the first few years and then cobbled something together quickly; it implies that after tenure the librarian will do little or no scholarship. A few smaller items scattered around the timeline and one or two meatier items later shows a progression or at least some activity throughout the librarian's time at the institution.

Fairly often there is a progression to scholarship. One might start by giving a talk or hosting a poster session at a conference. That might lead to a more involved article. That article might inspire a second research project on a related topic. Each bit of research is an individual asset and should be counted as such. For example, if someone regularly reads or reviews individual books and realizes that several of these have common themes, she might pull those together into a longer review article or bibliographic essay. As noted in an earlier chapter, efficient people take notes on what they read. This is one reason why. Looking back over that inventory might show a cluster of books on a topic or related in some way. A quick re-read of those titles, along with one or two more recent titles on the same subject or theme could provide sufficient material for a long (or even a short) review article or bibliographic essay, or enough source material for a presentation or poster session. Someone who edits a newsletter might sense a theme in recent submissions or note a recurring theme when talking with colleagues or reading email chains. That might lead to a newsletter article or a longer article published elsewhere. Writing up brief conference reports or tweeting conferences in real time might lead you to notice how two presentations compared/contrasted which might lead to a newsletter article on the consensus/two schools of thought, which might in turn lead to a longer article.

5.1 Research

Not all presentations and publications are research related, and there is a discussion on various types of publications and presentation further long in the chapter, but let us go over some of the aspects of a research study just to cover the basics, and then go into ways this research might be used. Some job-related tasks or committee work involve doing some kind of research and some graduate library schools do not include a research component, so a brief overview might be helpful.

New projects always start with a general thought, "I wonder ..." "I wonder if other librarians have the same problem and if so how have they solved it. Several of the books I've recently read have a similar theme, I wonder if there are others like it. I noticed this interesting tidbit in an article I read and wonder if there is other research out there on that topic. This is a really interesting article but the research was done several years ago, has anyone updated it? No? Maybe someone should do that. Maybe that person should be me." Combing back through notes of books read or links to online articles that sparked an inquisitive thought are other ways of finding a research interest. Librarians who do not have a flexible schedule or generous time allotment for research should look around their desks and see what they are working on that might make an interesting presentation or article. If most of your time is spent doing freshman instruction you might find an old folder or box full of outdated handouts or some bits of clear plastic your senior colleagues tell you are overhead transparencies (something new librarians have probably never have heard of). Looking through those and asking friends at other institutions and instructional clearinghouses for other examples of disused instructional materials could lead to a poster session, presentation, or article on how technology has changed instruction. Or has it? Are we still using the same examples, teaching the same search strategies or are we doing something entirely new? Are we as focused on using controlled vocabulary or was it lost along the way, and if so when and why?

Nonwork aspects of life are also a great way of developing research projects. Knowing that time is one's most valuable asset means looking for ways to maximize time spent. This is especially true for people with family responsibilities. I developed a research project based on a series of videos I watched over and over again with my children. The videos were retellings of classic children's fairy tales with a cgi Barbie character as the focal point. The stories were given a more feminist cast than usual and the research project involved studying the male protagonist in relation to standard gendered roles. It was initially a paper at a regional conference and then expanded into a journal article.

Everyone gets ideas for research or wonders about things. One of the primary differences between people who get ideas and people who follow through with them and write or present on them is record keeping. Yes, success or failure is often dependent, once again, on a good filing system and jotting down notes. Most of us have the occasional slow afternoon or know the frustration of waiting for a phone call and not being able to get anything done until the call comes through. Or perhaps there is a short thirty minute time period between meetings. Those short time slots are a great time to begin a research project. The first step is always looking to see if anyone else has written on the topic and what data might already be available. This usually takes the form of a literature review and/or an online search. Save the results, in electronic or print form, and put them in a physical or digital folder labeled with the research idea, and set it aside. Maybe this lit review will spark some questions about which way the research will go, or discover that multiple studies have been done on the topic already, but a review article or bibliographic essay would be a good addition to the topic.

On another slow afternoon or between meetings there will be time to type up some research notes, the beginnings of a rough outline or a written formal literature review. A month or so later on another late Friday afternoon or when a meeting was canceled, plan out a research study or start to design a power point for a conference talk. In this way a project builds slowly, sort of sneaking up in bits and pieces, so that when it is time to start a new research project, one is already begun, even better if there are several to choose from. Having a series of "half-baked" ideas means never starting from scratch. When one project is completed, simply peruse the folders of possible research projects and pick the one that suits that day's mood or that semester's/year's time frame. For some projects, timeliness is not an issue and so a project folder can move from job to job or stay in a file cabinet for years until it feels right or perhaps a likely collaborator comes along. The longest I have kept a project folder, occasionally updating it, is roughly twenty-five years, through four jobs in three states, from the initial idea to an article being written and accepted. This may seem, and perhaps is, far too long to let an idea cogitate, but it just never seemed like quite the right time, until it did, and then the process went rather quickly. Having a backlog of possible projects allows for a lot of flexibility. If one project involves reading a lot of background material or comparing a number of published works, reading a few here and there and taking good notes allows the work to be spread out over time so that it does not become tedious or overwhelming. Again, the finished project sort of sneaks up on you. It allows the researcher to pick whatever tickles his or her fancy at the moment, to choose a project that can be finished quickly or to start a longer project if time allows. Perhaps one project would be a wonderful peer-reviewed journal article and another a short conference paper or a quick poster session, to be expanded upon later. The trick is to start project folders as ideas occur, with a lit review and maybe some notes, and build as time allows. Having an assortment of projects to pick from is a luxury that less-organized colleagues do not have. They are perennially staring at blank sheets of paper or blinking cursors and wondering what on earth to do. The organized are ready and can, at times, win friends and gain influence by passing off an idea folder that is no longer as interesting as it once was, thus saving a colleague a lot of initial time and frustration.

A set of idea folders is also a great way to spur a collaboration. Say you are chatting with a friend at a conference or online and you both want to go to an upcoming conference or have to publish. Your friend may have interests or skills that would be really helpful in doing the research for one of your ideas, maybe they are really good at making graphs and charts, a talent you lack, and one of your ideas would require the results to be displayed that way. You can suggest the two of you work on that and if your friend agrees you can send them the information in your folder and off you go.

Procrastinators may find themselves starting lots of folders and perhaps even getting to the draft stage, but never really finishing. For some, the writing is the easy part and the process of preparing a presentation or formatting a manuscript for electronic submission is just too many details to manage. If this is a problem ask a colleague or a mentor or even a family member to nag you about it, with a self-set deadline to complete something. The perfect can be the enemy of the good. Fairly often a scholar is not really satisfied with a project, but a submission deadline or a conference date comes up and they just send it off. In my case I tend to dither until a deadline is close or, more often, I get more interested in another project and finish the first one so I can start on the next. The first project becomes sort of a blocked toothpaste tube that just has to be squeezed out.

For some just the idea of doing research is daunting, even though most people with a graduate or even an undergraduate degree have done some kind of research and written a lengthy paper. It is possible to approach more experienced scholars and ask if there is an idea you could develop together, an apprenticeship if you will. Or at least someone to talk through ideas with, to plan out a research strategy. An official mentor at a tenure-track institution might fill this role. If there is no such program or, for whatever reason, that person is not someone you feel comfortable with, ask someone else at your institution, or a librarian at another institution who has publishing experience. As someone who has published frequently, I have received emails and letters out of the blue from newer librarians who had a question about scholarship or about publishing in a particular area. As much as possible I have tried to answer those questions or point the person in a helpful direction. When I was a new librarian and just getting started I asked more experience librarians for advice, which most were happy to provide.

Scholarly research generally has a starting question or statement. It might be "does culture affect online search strategy?" or "What are standard features on library web pages?" or "Have librarians been used as study populations in social science research?" (These are all the starting question for articles I have published.) Again it is a good idea to have a general elevator speech or sentence summarizing the research project. If it cannot be distilled down into something understandable then perhaps it is not yet ready to be studied. If you do not understand what you are studying or cannot convey it in its simplest form to someone else you need to think about it more before starting.

Once the general concept is set, then it is a matter of finding the right research parameters. In one of the examples above, does culture affect online search strategy, the researcher would need to decide how culture would be defined. In that particular case the study populations were librarians in four different English-speaking countries. Each was sent a sample question and asked to prepare a search strategy to find articles on that topic. All would use the same language, which would remove the possibility of translation, and since the researcher was fluent only in English that was sort of a necessity. This is what is called an independent variable. This does not change. Other independent variables in this study were the type of institution (those with a degree in sociology), the database (sociological abstracts) and the search question. This helped ensure that the librarian doing the search, where possible the social science librarian was approached, could be expected to have some familiarity with the database and subject. These were uniform across all of the search subjects. The library web page study also had independent variables: all the libraries were academic libraries with websites.

In starting a research project it is important to decide early on what the independent variables will be. This can be one of those late afternoon/meeting was canceled activities that go into a folder for future use. Suppose a librarian is wondering whether or not books in a particular subject area are checked out more frequently when a class is taught in that subject. After all, we purchase books assuming they will be used to support the curriculum and, indeed, purchase particular subjects in particular levels of intensity and depth based on the curriculum. So, is that actually what happens? What would one need to research that?

Initially, the librarian might want to do a literature search to make sure someone else has not done the exact same study recently. If a similar study was done some years ago it could be updated. As a point of etiquette, when updating a previous study, contact the initial researchers to ask if they plan on updating the study or if they are aware of anyone else doing so. Other types of background research are to see generally what had been published on book ordering and collection use relating to the curriculum, to become acquainted with professional thought on the topic, and to provide the literature review for the article if the study actually becomes an article or a presentation.

Then move on to data. First off, is historical circulation data available? Not on which individuals had checked books out, but whether or not specific books had been checked out, and when. Without that data there would not be any way to do the study. Is it possible to run a circulation report on specific call number ranges? A corollary to this is whether or not it is possible to tell if the book had been checked out locally or if it had been borrowed via interlibrary loan. After all, without that data the test results could be skewed. It might be possible to get general interlibrary loan data, to see overall what percentage of circulation was internal versus external. If it is a small percentage overall that could be noted in the study results.

Secondly, data on classes taught over the test period would be needed. What classes had been offered and when. Then particular classes and book classifications would need to be selected. Vague interdisciplinary classes or very broad overview courses would be too scattershot; it would be impossible to pin down a particular part of the collection that would be affected. Would the researcher want to limit to one department and select a handful of classes from that department or select classes from a variety of departments? At this point a research strategy comes into play.

Often times a research project plays out over more than one individual piece of scholarship. This is not to get to the level of "least publishable unit" but to take into account what can be dealt with or expressed in a standard journal article or book chapter (we will assume at this point no one is going after an entire book) or paper presentation. So this project, and really any project, can be divided into one or more projects. Initially, the research might be done on one particular department. Slicing down to one individual professor could be tricky unless that person was a co-author; there could be personal issues otherwise. So, let us say a department is selected, and a handful of classes over a two- or three-year period, taught by a variety of people. Another factor to consider would whether or not these classes had a research component? Naturally, this could affect the research outcome, so that would be another variable to contend with. Let us limit further to classes with a research component, perhaps a methods class with a consistent research requirement that has a different focus depending on who is teaching it. The focus of any one class would need to have a notable connection to a particular part of the collection, one that could be defined by a call number range small enough to work with but large enough to have a sufficient number of books to provide adequate data. This would be the first part of a larger research study. Once this part was done another department could be selected and those research results compared to this one, as second publication/presentation project. Perhaps then the librarian could find a partner at another school who would replicate the research at his or her school to provide comparative data. Perhaps they might want to compare honors and nonhonors sections of the same classes, or look at lower level and upper level classes, or graduate and undergraduate classes. So the initial idea brings forth more than one research opportunity.

Once the variables in the initial study are set, the librarian finds control data, something to compare the test data to, for example, a year in which no classes were being taught on that subject. There would be other possible factors, such as a graduate student doing thesis or dissertation work on that subject, and that could influence the results. If the researcher could not pin down a subject area that could be effectively studied the idea would need to be set aside until this design flaw could be settled, or perhaps the study could be shifted from books to an online dataset or a database that the library makes available, one that was specific enough to be used by one or two classes at a time and then not used the next semester.

But let us assume the librarian could find a portion of the book collection, database, or dataset, and one or more classes that would be sufficient to work with, and to circulation or download data. Then it is a simple matter of comparing time stamped spreadsheet data, to see if there is a bump in circulation during the semester the class is taught, and then this research repeated for the other classes/subject areas being studied. If there is no notable difference between the semesters before and after the class is taught (and several semesters before and after would make the research stronger), then the conclusion is that either students or faculty at that institution research that subject regularly, or that students do not use the library collection for that project. Then the question becomes what do they use for their research, and perhaps looking at interlibrary loan records for that semester would provide an answer. Possibly the librarian could ask one of the instructors teaching that class if he or she would be willing to let the librarian look at class papers, or at least their bibliographies, to see what resources students are using. If some of the library's collections are in remote storage or if there is direct patron borrowing from consortium partners it might be possible to get circulation data on books in that specific call number range from those libraries or library collections as well. That could, in fact, make up another publication/presentation aspect of the larger research strategy.

Each research project will have independent variables and controls. It could be the type and size of library. As I am at an academic library most of my research projects have been limited to academic libraries, though they may vary in size and type, community college libraries versus university libraries, undergraduate versus graduate programs, and so on. Sometimes a research project will start with an examination of something at one type of library and then grow into a comparison of that data with another type of library. But all projects have parameters. That is the first thing to set.

Each idea needs to be thought through with an eye to setting the project structure, what is being tested, where and how. Even ideas that do not involve studying statistics need parameters. In a review of multiple books, all those books need to have common ties, or be interconnected. A survey of books on a particular topic would need some form of coding sheet, with a way to note where specific topics were addressed, and a system for tracking compare/contrast data. Detailed journal literature reviews, comparing several articles on a subject will need similar data tools.

Empirical studies, such as the one outlined above on the impact of course focus on collection use, will produce data and numerical results. This will need to be formatted in a way that people can understand it, not only in words but also in graphs, charts, and the like. A college course in statistics can come in very handy in situations like that, or at least some proficiency with a software package like Microsoft's Excel. Someone with a keen grasp of statistics and an ability to create the proper numerical supporting images for a research project can wrangle that into co-authorships or simply make a lot of friends, depending on the level of involvement required.

Although the "I wonder ..." method of finding a research topic is a frequent, useful, and effective one, there are others. One is the "What do I have that others may not?" method. In the chapter on counting assets, one section was on knowing who you are and what strengths or assets you have. I am an armchair politico; my idea of a good time on a Saturday night is reviewing campaign finance reports. Not a lot of librarians (or people generally) share this inclination. So I have written and presented on librarians and politics, and how librarians can influence their elected officials; these offerings met with some success in large part because there was not a lot of competition for space on the topic. Efforts on more mainstream library topics were passed over (articles rejected, presentation abstracts not accepted), probably because there were more, and no doubt better, options to choose from. Librarian John Maxymuk likes football. That may not be unusual but he does not just like to watch it, he studies it, and has written books analyzing teams by who wore what jersey number. This has gotten him quoted in the *New York Times* and other national publications. As mentioned before, in the land of the blind the one-eyed man is the king. A librarian just back from maternity leave (or hoping to go out on maternity leave in a year or so) might do a study on library leave policies. Someone with elder parent issues might survey librarians in similar situations. Both would, of course, need to follow institutional rules on human subjects research. As previously mentioned, I once gave a paper and later wrote an article on the male protagonist in a series of children's videos, simply because I had watched them so often with my own children. Likewise when my children were older and very involved in scouts (and thus I was very involved with scouts), I researched older editions of scout leader handbooks and gave a conference paper on national scouting organization's evolving view of parental involvement. At some point in the distant future, I may do an in-depth literature review of scholarship on the role of grandparents in developing a child's love of reading.

In the previous chapter on librarianship there was a discussion of volunteering to be the in-house expert on a new system, database, or technology. Or simply becoming the in-house expert whether one wanted to or not. This level of expertise is another gateway to research. Writing or presenting on a topic early is a good way to become cited, that is to have people cite your research. It may be brilliant work on your part, but even if it is not, if it is the only work on there on the topic it is likely to be cited. Hockey player Wayne Gretzky is famous for a quote, provided in differing ways in different sources, that a good hockey player goes where the puck is; a great hockey player goes where the puck is going to be. In other words, get out front. Being in the vanguard is a wonderful career strategy, but the vanguard is usually short lived. Other players will pass you by, but this is a move that can be used to build momentum for other career aspects. Fortunately librarianship, unlike hockey, is not dependent on winning the game, so writing about a product or resource that does not last still counts as writing, as long as it is published or formally presented.

Rejection is a sad but ever present factor in the life of a tenure-track librarian, or any librarian who intends to share some aspect of research with the larger world. Papers will be turned down, article manuscripts rejected. There is no way to soften the blow. It stings. It brings forth strong emotions and impolite language. There is no way around this. The thing to remember is that it is not personal; granted that does not really help soften the blow, but none of it is directed at the person as a person. It is merely words on paper, and usually conferences and journals receive far more submissions than they can possibly accept. If time allows wait a few weeks and then send it off again to someone else; if time does not allow for a mourning period, read over the piece to see if there are glaring errors not noticed the first time, and send it off elsewhere. Or, another option is to put that particular manuscript or abstract back in a folder and file it away for a later time; then take another research folder out and start again. There may be a way to re-use the data in the rejected article in a future research project. The ever present possibility of rejection is another reason to start planning early. If you have two projects in the works and one is turned down by the first journal you submitted it to, you still have time to submit it elsewhere, and you still have the other project to work on. If you devote all of your pre-tenure time and attention to one article, finish writing it in the year before you go up for review, and it is rejected, you are in a very stressful position.

While starting a folder can be done is snippets of time here and there, full research projects require longer stretches of dedicated time. Even an hour or two a week, though longer periods are better, can go a long way toward finishing a project. Some people set aside time every week, say the last 2 hours of the day on Friday afternoons. Or the first 2 hours on Monday, or on an extended break between two weekend reference desk shifts. It can be hard to set aside this time when the demands of daily work life seem more urgent. Just keep telling yourself that if you are on tenure-track this IS part of your job. If it is difficult to do this during the school year, concentrate on semester breaks or summer, setting aside 90 minutes or 2 hours each day or one afternoon a week. For those who want to prepare for a future tenure-track position or just be a more viable candidate if such a position becomes available, and research time is not possible during the standard work schedule, getting up early on Saturday or Sunday, or staying up late is a strategy, This is not necessarily a lot of fun, but in some situations it is unavoidable. Think of the research project as your temporary hobby.

5.2   Speaking

Fear of public speaking is supposedly second only to the fear of death. Some reports say that fear of public speaking is greater than a fear of death. Either way it looms large on the horizon, and not in a good way. The standard advice, imagining the audience naked or in their underwear, is not especially helpful, particularly in an era of an aging population. For people who wear eyeglasses simply taking them off to speak can be useful, as the audience becomes one large pleasantly impressionistic blur. In those cases it is best to be seated or to keep one hand on the podium to avoid getting too close to the edge of the stage. The easiest way to reduce the fear of public speaking is to imagine that someone has asked you to explain something, a friend or younger colleague over lunch; the audience is your lunch partner. You are simply telling them something, or reading a story to a child. Most of us have had to give a presentation in college or a report to a work group or read aloud to one or more fidgety toddlers. A conference presentation is no more than that, just to a slightly different audience.

Practicing can be a way of building confidence. Try out your presentation for a group of friends or colleagues to test it out. If you have a research group or an informal group of other new hires across the library or across campus, ask if you can practice for them as well. The more you give the presentation the more comfortable you will be with it. Even practicing in your living room for your cat or in the shower will help you feel more at ease. Susan Reinhart's *Giving Academic Presentations* is a good overview of how to prepare a successful presentation.

A smaller form of conference presentation is a poster session. This can be thought of as an adult science fair. Someone brings a trifold poster board or other presentation form; it could be a laptop PowerPoint show or some other type of visual aid. The person hosting the poster session sits in their designated area as people walk by and answers questions about their presentation. This is often an effective way of getting feedback on initial research findings or doing a "show and tell" or "how we did it good" report on something at your library or institution. Enterprising graduate students might put together a poster session based on a research paper or internship project. Not all conferences have poster sessions, but for those that do it can be a good way for someone new to ease into giving presentations or for experienced scholars to do something a little less stressful.

While the inclination is to think of presentations at large national conferences, there are a number of other, smaller, opportunities. The trick here is to review a call for papers site. The University of Pennsylvania maintains a large list of calls for papers. This is simply the initial request for papers that a planned conference sends out. There are association conferences, subject-oriented conferences, regional group conferences, and all sorts of conferences. Some want long papers, some want short, some offer the opportunity for poster sessions.

This can be very important for people whose family responsibilities or financial situations or lack of institutional support prevent them from traveling far afield to the usual national conferences. Of course, being near metropolitan areas is a big help because more conferences are likely to be held there, but even smaller university or college towns will host something once in a while. There are even online conferences that are conducted in a completely virtual environment. There is no harm in reaching a bit, submitting an abstract to a conference that seems like a stretch. A conference that receives two or three times as many abstracts as they have slots will disappoint a lot of people, but someone will be accepted. Smaller or less well-known conferences sometimes have difficulty filling spots. One never knows. The only sure bet is that someone who never submits an abstract will never be accepted.

The usual process is that a conference sends out a call for papers, with a description of the conference, some general subject guidelines, a suggested abstract length, submission process instructions, and details on the conference, when and where it will be held. Some conferences will have online submission forms; more commonly people send in abstracts via email. People interested in presenting will submit their abstract (summary of their talk) and then wait to hear. Abstracts need not be overly detailed. It is not necessary for the person submitting to have already done the research. Some abstracts will be on an experiment or research that is already in progress or is expected to be done by the time of the conference, but it is not unusual for the research to not actually be completed until/unless the paper is accepted. For people who work best with a deadline it is often the only way research is completed; they have to give a paper so they better have something to say.

Some conferences will accept full panel submissions. This means instead of sending in one single paper a group will band together and submit a number of related papers that form a theme. This saves the organizer the trouble of grouping together individual abstracts into panel sessions. Getting a panel together is a wonderful way to keep in touch with colleagues and friends at other institutions. For example, a former graduate school study group, now all employed at different institutions, might find a conference that relates to their graduate school subject, and submit a panel presentation in hopes of having a reunion at the conference, perhaps at their institutions' expense. It can also be a great way to make new friends. For example, having read an article that is related to your research, you might contact the author of that article to ask if they would be interested in being on a panel. If you present a paper at one conference and know that in the next year another conference you want to attend is coming up, see if there are a couple of speakers at the first conference who might be interested in putting together a panel for the second conference. For example, I gave a paper at a conference on cycling history about a project I had been working on, digitizing bike routes published in a newspaper in 1897 and 1898. Another paper at that conference, like mine, touched on the economics of bicycles and cycling during the cycling boom of the late 1800s. A third speaker was not an economic historian but a friend of his, attending but not speaking, was. The three of us decided to think about submitting a panel on the business side of cycling in the 19th century to a conference on economic history. It might be a stretch, but it was a good way to meet new people. Contact librarians at neighboring institutions to see if they want to submit a paper (even if it is not part of a panel) and carpool to save money. Having friends around or nearby can reduce anxiety and provide travel companions. Another way to cut costs or combine business and pleasure is to look for conferences near where friends and family live. Staying with them would cut down on travel costs and allow you to visit while you are there.

If a conference runs over multiple days it is acceptable to ask that you not be scheduled on a specific day. Your request might not be granted, and, depending on the mood of the conference organizer, and how many such requests he has received, can count against you. In cases like this a familiarity with the conference and how it is run comes in handy. Ask around and see if anyone you know has gone in previous years and what their experiences have been. However, if there are unavoidable conflicts (family wedding, final exam, and child's graduation) on a day of the conference it can be good to state that up front, to avoid having to withdraw later. Sometimes one can bargain. A conference that has multiple concurrent sessions is often on the lookout for moderators, especially at undesirable times. So, for instance, someone submitting an abstract to a three-day conference with multiple concurrent sessions, with a conflict on the first day, might include a note with the abstract or in a separate email to the conference organizer after the abstract is accepted, that she cannot be present the first day, but would be available to moderate a panel on the second and third day including the 8:00 am sessions and the last session of the conference. Traditionally moderators introduce the speakers, make sure speakers stay within their time frame, and introduce the question and answer session at the end of the panel. Moderating is more service than scholarship, but it can still be listed in a tenure or promotion packet. It might also be possible to move a presentation if a conflict comes up later, but this is rare and the person asking should have a good reason for doing so.

What many people fear is that someone in the audience will stand up and shout "You're wrong!" or "You do not know what you are talking about!" I have never seen or heard about that happening, outside of fiction. What might happen is that an audience member will ask the speaker if he or she is familiar with a work that contradicts what the speaker has said. In those cases an "I'm not familiar with that work. Thank you! I will look into it" takes care of it. Sometimes commenters can ask questions in an unartful manner, but it only reflects on them. Librarians tend to be well behaved and even when speakers make outrageous statements the audience will sit quietly. Another fear is of having a meltdown on stage or of making an embarrassing mistake. People do make mistakes. Everyone does, sometimes at a podium or in front of an audience. They simply continue on, sometimes blissfully unaware. Sometimes equipment malfunctions. People do the best they can and the audience understands. Anyone who has gone to a number of conferences will have seen speakers make mistakes. One example is someone who held up a picture and said "I wish there was some way I could show this to everyone." There is—scan it and make it part of a PowerPoint or other visual presentation. This was said by someone on a panel with speakers who had made PowerPoint presentations. People might have quietly thought he was making a somewhat odd statement, but no one said anything and the presentation went on. In general, people do not remember the names of presenters after the presentation has ended and they have gone on to the next item on the agenda.

A joke sometimes heard at conferences is that even if no one shows up at a presentation the speaker can still put it on their vita and promotion documents. British academic novelist David Lodge parodied the fear of speaking in his novel *A Small World* when scholar Rodney Wainwright has writer's block and cannot finish a talk that he is scheduled to give at a conference. He simply cannot find the words and gets up to give his talk when it is only half finished, hoping for a miracle which arrives in an unusual form; someone comes in and says there is a suspected case of Legionnaire's Disease at the hotel and the audience scatters (Lodge, 1984, p. 347). An unprepared speaker cannot count on an epidemic to save the day; having a complete, rehearsed talk is the best bulwark against disaster. But it is true that a paper presented at a conference before an audience of three looks the same on a vita as a paper presented before an audience of 300.

As for general speaking tips, there are some standards. It is better to talk casually than to read a written paper. That gets rather dull for the audience. Having notes or talking points on a screen are acceptable and almost ubiquitous, but simply standing at a podium and reading is to be avoided if possible. Make eye contact with the audience, or, if that is uncomfortable, find a spot on the back wall just above the line of the audiences' heads and focus on that. Some speakers try to make eye contact with a number of people, others chose one and visually return to that person multiple times. Regardless of the method, looking up and smiling while talking is always good.

Timing one's talk can prevent the cardinal sin of presenting—especially when on a panel or shared space—going over one's time. Each person on a panel or shared presentation has a set number of minutes. Even in a single speaker session there is a time limit. A speaker who says "Well the audience seemed to enjoy my talk so I kept going" is doing a disservice to later speakers. Their full talks might have been as well received, but the audience will never know as there would not be time to hear them. Going over time means that someone else would not have their set amount of time and will have to shorten their talk, or that people will be late to the next session or would not have time for the all-important coffee or bathroom break. One sign of a mature speaker is that he or she can adjust to whatever circumstances arise, shortening or lengthening a talk as needed. Newer speakers may mistime their remarks because they speak more quickly due to nervousness (a partial solution is to write "slow down" or "breathe" in the margins of written notes or between paragraphs of written remarks). Some people get sidetracked by stories and go longer than planned. While most people use cell phones as their timepiece these days, it is a good idea to have a watch on the podium or table next to you to track your time as you go. Most conferences will provide time keepers that will give a sign when 5 min remains of the speaker's time. If possible read the mood of the audience and adjust remarks as needed. If the audience is restless in one part of a talk go quickly through it and on to the next. New speakers are always a bit nervous, but with practice become a little better at being comfortable speaking in front of a group and adjusting to situations on the fly.

Most talks include a question and answer session. Answer questions as fully but succinctly as you can, offering to reply in more detail if the questioner will supply an email address. There are standard answers to people who disagree with you or give long comments with no real question:

"I never thought of it that way; interesting point. Are there any other questions?"
"You've given me a lot to think about."
"I haven't read the book/article you are referring to but will certainly look into it."
"I read that, too, but interpreted it differently."
"We will just have to disagree."

If someone says "… but that goes against what you wrote…" ask them to cite which publication and what section or page numbers they are referring to.

If you have no idea what the person is talking about, simply say "thank you" and go on to the next question.

If someone insists on asking repeated and sharp questions either the speaker or the moderator should ask them to allow others a chance to ask questions.

Celebrity is rare among academics, especially librarians, but there are some aspects of it that people who give presentations sometimes encounter. Many conferences will have a speaker's ribbon on the name badge of people who will be giving presentations. This is a conversation starter. Fellow presenters will ask about your talk and share details of theirs, even if only when and where the talks will take place. People who are not presenting may ask about your talk. Similar to the elevator speech mentioned earlier, it is a good idea to have a quick summation of your talk, a sentence or two that can be used on occasions like this. If someone asks a speaker what they will be talking about and that person cannot provide a succinct description, it is a bad sign. An identifiable speaker sitting alone at lunch or standing alone at a coffee break might find themselves approached by conference attendees looking for someone to talk with. It is a good icebreaker. The person asks you about your talk, you ask them about their job, how they are enjoying the conference, etc.

After a panel or presentation, it is common for people to approach a speaker with further questions or comments. This should always be taken as a good sign and the speaker should remember to bring business cards to hand out to people with whom they might wish to keep in touch with (for future collaborations if nothing else). At times it is simply a matter of a member of the audience for whom the conference experience becomes more real or satisfactory if they have personal contact with a speaker. In that case very little is required of the speaker other than to be pleasant. If someone says they enjoyed your talk, thank them and tell this it is kind of them to let you know. Ask them how they are enjoying the conference. This is not an opportunity to go off on a monolog about the details of your research; save that in case someone actually asks. At the end of the conversation, or as a way of ending it, thank the person for coming to your talk and say that you do not want to keep them from the next session. If the person you are talking with is a senior scholar, jot down their name as a possible outside reviewer.

However, at times people will ask for details or inquire further about conclusions, or if you have plans for further research. If the room is needed for the next panel session, see if the conversation can continue in the hallway or if time and schedules allow set up a future meeting or ask them to email you. This can be a great way to get ideas for further research or find a collaborator for future project or panel session, or simply get another perspective on the issue. If the conversation becomes uncomfortable for any reason, plead another obligation and end it.

In the audience it can seem like every (or most) speakers are experts on their topic, all knowing, walking encyclopedias, or research geniuses. Anyone who has given a conference presentation knows this is not the case. Okay, there may be a few outliers who do fit that description, but for the most part speakers are nervous, hoping all goes well, and perhaps tweaking their talk at the last minute. This is normal.

Giving talks can be a lot of fun and is a great way to get feedback on research projects and to get ideas for continuing that research. It is also a great way to meet people with similar interests. If you think the presentation might make a good article someday, Furstenberg suggests writing a full speech or draft article before preparing a visual presentation, so that some of the hard work will already be done, otherwise it is too easy to let speaking notes and slides sit idle once the conference is over (Furstenberg, 2013).

5.3   Writing/Publishing

Anyone who has been to graduate school, or written intensive undergraduate research papers can write an article. Often a long research paper is about the length of a substantial article manuscript. Anyone who has written a master's level thesis or an undergraduate honors thesis should be able to do the research and write up an article or a book chapter.

There are various schools of thought on how to prepare a manuscript. One important factor is what type of manuscript is being prepared; is it a newsletter article, a peer-reviewed journal article, a book chapter, or something else. Sometimes it is a matter of matching a folder or idea with an opportunity. In the previous section, on presenting I mentioned watching calls for papers. These can be for publications as well as conference presentations. So, someone watching a calls site might see a call for a special issue of a journal and the theme dovetails nicely with an idea or a partially formed research project already in a folder. If the deadline can be met, it could be a great opportunity. Or perhaps the call is for an edited monograph, and you wrote an article on that topic that was recently rejected by a journal. It becomes an excellent opportunity to do a quick rewrite for the new venture. Or perhaps a friend or colleague emails to say he or she is editing a journal issue or a book and is looking for material, or writes a newsletter and needs an article to replace one whose author had to drop out at the last minute. Then the decision is an easy one.

But, most of the time there is some intent in starting on what type of manuscript is being prepared. New librarians or librarians newly hired on a tenure-track line might be looking for a quick publication just to get something on their vita, to provide a little breathing room for a longer research piece. People who have never published before, like people who have never presented before, can easily assume that only the smartest, most special people get to do that. Again, this is in incorrect belief. Generally speaking those who are published are those who submit manuscripts. People who insist on perfection submit fewer manuscripts than those who merely aim to do a good job. Social media and online journals have blurred some of the lines between types of publications. Do not assume that if you host a widely read and respected online site that it will count as scholarly activity. Talk with senior colleagues and get their impressions; ask around and see if other people have counted digital projects and online endeavors as scholarship. For the purposes of this book we are looking at more traditional publishing ventures, though some of those might be online. Here are some easy ways to get started.

Book reviews—chances are every librarian enjoys reading. A good way for people who have never published to get comfortable with the idea of seeing their name in print, meeting deadlines, and working within a suggested word count, is to write book reviews. Any librarian who orders books is familiar with book review journals. Those reviews are written by someone; why should not that someone be you? Contact those publications with a vita or list of interests and qualifications and a cover letter. This should not take up research time, but instead use your standard reading time to read books that can be reviewed. Find a subject that you enjoy reading so this is folded in to your regular schedule. Reviewers frequently get advanced copies and it can be exciting to know you are reading a book before all but a few others see it. This also lets you see trends and research areas before the general public sees them. This puts you in the vanguard and allows you to develop your own research, informed by what you are reading. "But wait," you say, "I'm reviewing mysteries; how would that lead to research?" Are there trends in detective personalities? Are you seeing a lot of Scandinavian writers? Are there standard features that never change? The answers to these questions could lead to a longer review article.

In addition to the standard book review journals, most scholarly and professional publications have book reviews. The reviews in those publications are longer and more involved, more scholarly. Some of these journals have separate book review editors; you can contact those editors expressing interest in reviewing. Some journals have lists of books they want reviewed, others let people ask to review specific books. You might be asked for a writing sample or a summary of your qualifications and interests. The top journals are less likely to have reviewer spots open, but it never hurts to ask.

Book reviews would not get you tenure, but they are a good way to get professional credit for something you do anyway. Writing reviews can also lead to research ideas. People who are unfamiliar with the culture and habit of writing (making time for it, working with publisher guidelines, and so on) can use writing book reviews as a way to get more comfortable with it.

Review publications usually want short reviews, a paragraph. Articles in standard journals might be anywhere from a paragraph to a few pages.

Newsletters—there will be more on this in the next chapter, on service, but most professional associations have newsletters and most are usually looking for copy. So are smaller professional or subject-oriented newsletters. If you have read a book or attended a conference that would be of interest to readers of that newsletter, email the editor and ask if they would like a brief article on it. Like book reviews, writing newsletter articles will not get you tenure, but it is a good way of getting your name out there and, also like, reviews, newsletter articles can sometimes lead to bigger and better publishing projects. For example, a quick review of a new online product could lead to a longer journal article on how that product compares to other, similar products. Newsletter articles are usually less than a page long.

Those are also great places to start for the new or nervous writer. More experienced writers might wish to keep a hand in writing reviews or conference reports. However, they will want to move on to more substantial publications. Professional blogs might be regarded in the same way that a newsletter would, depending on the level of sophistication of the blog or site.

Professional journals—not every publication is scholarly or peer reviewed. Some are intended as professional literature, something like *American Libraries*, *College & Research Library News*, or *Library Hi-Tech News* with information of interest to people in a particular line of work. These publications are often more news based than research based. This is what makes them valuable—the information gets to you quicker and in a more timely fashion than research articles. Professional journals are great places to publish short pieces on new technologies or new ways of doing thing. It is the place to announce new developments, interview people who have done something innovative or interesting, and other news-related material. Professional journals are also often interested in book reviews, summaries of journal articles, and conference reports. Again, this is a good way to get your feet wet in publishing, and also to demonstrate that you are ahead of the curve with something. The length of articles in these journals varies greatly.

Nonpeer-reviewed journals—not all journals are peer reviewed. Some simply have an editor who makes the publication decision. It is a body of one. These journals can still publish very good work, even good research. However, in most tenure-track institutions these journals are not as highly regarded as a peer-reviewed journal. Check to see what the rules are for your individual institution. Even at institutions that prefer peer-reviewed publications, an article in a quality nonpeer-reviewed journal can still look good in a packet, as part of a body of work. How do you know if a journal is peer reviewed? It should be mentioned on the journal's website or in the journal itself. If not, ask the editor.

Peer-reviewed journals—What is peer review? It means that a group of people, known as reviewers or referees, who have some knowledge of the subject of your manuscript look it over and make a suggestion or decision on whether it should be published, be revised and then published, heavily revised and resubmitted, or not accepted. This is to ensure that the research is done correctly and the overall concept makes sense. A good copyeditor can catch typos and grammatical errors. A good reviewer will note that the name of an important person in that field (but unknown to just about everyone else) is misspelled or that a significant piece of recent published research is not included in the bibliography or mentioned in the article. A good peer reviewer will understand what the author is intending, the theoretical framework behind it, and whether or not the research design is supportable. An article on a specific product or database will hopefully be refereed by someone who is familiar with it. There are usually three reviewers, though there may be more. Most journals will respond to a manuscript submission in 6–8 weeks, perhaps sooner, with a decision. If an author had not heard in that time it is acceptable to send a note to the editor asking about the article's status. A request for revisions should not be taken as a rejection—it is not. The reviewers liked the article, but felt it could be better with some changes. It can be frustrating if the reviewer comments conflict. In that case simply make as many changes as you can and, if you like, explain to the editor why you were not able to make the others. A request to re-write and re-submit expresses interest in the topic and the article, but shows sufficient concern that a major restructuring is needed. If you do not want to do all the work requested you can do minor changes and submit elsewhere. A rejection is hard to take; rejection is never fun. In this case, though, it merely means that the material can either be submitted elsewhere or put back into storage to be revised for another publication or repurposed for something else at a later date.

Some blogs and online sites are peer reviewed, but these are few and far between. Check carefully on the status of online sites before putting publications there down as peer reviewed. Ask colleagues what they think of the publication or ask the editor about the publication's status.

Book chapters—Edited monographs have chapters with a common theme, but written by a variety of people. They are frequently the same length as a substantial journal article. Book editors often issue a call for papers and do not accept all answers to that call, but book chapters are not considered peer reviewed. In rare occasions book chapters are by invitation only. More commonly someone will line up people they know or know of to write chapters in the book and then go outside that circle to find people to write other chapters. Sometimes a book editor will simply issue a call for papers. One thing to watch for is the status of the books' publication. In some cases a publisher asks someone to put together a book, with an unofficial agreement to publish, sometimes an editor contacts a publisher with a general outline and is given provisional approval to prepare a manuscript. Those are promising situations. There are times when someone lines up contributors, or worse requests actual chapters, and then goes to publishers with a completed manuscript. The editor may take months to find a publisher or may not be able to find one at all. In that case your work on that chapter may be tied up for months or years, with no guarantee of publication. If approached about writing a book chapter or when replying to a call for papers for an edited book, ask whether or not the editor already has an arrangement with a publisher.

Books—the thought of writing an entire book is a frightening one. After all, who writes books? Smart people, talented people, certainly not the likes of you and me! And yet, here we are. People who write books are people who submit book proposals or who write enough that publishers contact them. There certainly is an overlap between intelligence, talent, and the wherewithal to publish and submit proposals, but it is incorrect to assume that book are written by the smartest most talented people out there. If the thought of writing 150 or 200 or more pages is off putting, break it down into pieces. Could you write 10 or 15 pages on one aspect of the subject? Yes? Then, could you write another 10 or 15 pages on another aspect? And so on, divide it into chapters and then subsections of chapters. It is much less frightening that way. Estimate roughly how many words you will want for each section and keep a spreadsheet of your progress.

Once you have some idea what type of publication you are aiming for, you will know the approximate length and depth you need to write. As noted above, some publications are looking for relatively brief submissions. Librarians, and academics generally, will build upon their past research and publications. For example, a brief note for a newsletter will lead to a longer article for a professional journal which will lead to a peer-reviewed article or a book chapter.

Let us focus on peer-reviewed articles as that is often what is most needed for tenure. It is a good idea to have a short list of journals that you would like to publish the article in, as that will give you a good idea how long and in what format to write. Some peer-reviewed journals are more literary or humanities focused. These have less charts and graphs, and often do not have an empirical research basis. Others are more science based and will have a standard research component. Some journals include both types of articles. Browsing the table of contents for the previous year or two of the journal will provide some idea of what types of articles are usually published there.

It is acceptable, sometimes advisable to contact an editor once an article is starting to take shape, and ask if they think it is something that might be suitable for their journal; this is called a query letter. This serves a variety of purposes. For one, it allows the editor to say that she do not think the article would suit. Granted most journals will have a website with submission guidelines, but sometimes these are rather vague. A query letter allows an editor to save you the trouble of submitting when the article is not really something they would be looking for; it saves the editor from sending an article through peer review when the response is most likely negative. It saves everyone time. Of course, a positive response to a query letter is not a guarantee of publication; manuscripts still have to go through peer review and it might be turned down for any number of reasons. A query letter also gives the editor a heads up that a manuscript on your topic might be forthcoming and this helps her in planning out what to send to which reviewer, or might allow her to group similar articles together in an issue or perhaps put them in sequential issues instead of the same issue. Some sample wording for a query letter might include the following:

Dear (editor's name)
I am working on an article manuscript and, given the submission guidelines on the (journal or publisher name) website, think it might be suitable for submission to (journal or publisher name). The article is on (brief description of the article; keep it to a few sentences at most). I know that any manuscript submitted would need to go through the peer review process before a decision is made, but if you can tell from the description that it is not the sort of thing your journal would be interested in, it would save you the time of sending it out for review. Thank you in advance for any guidance you might have.

Sincerely,

(your name)

A friendly editor in a good mood who is not interested in your topic might suggest other places for submission. Sometimes the response to a query letter will simply note that the journal has just accepted several articles on a similar subject and would not really want another one so quickly, suggesting you either submit elsewhere or not submit until a later date. This gives you the option of finishing another article first and then going back to this one, or submitting elsewhere.

Claire Renzetti, editor of the peer-reviewed journal *Violence Against Women*, suggests a more involved query letter:

More productive, I think, are queries that ask specific questions. Examples of such queries are: "My manuscript exceeds the page limit posted for submissions because it includes lengthy excerpted quotes from interviews. May I still submit it?" and "I noticed in perusing recent journal issues that none of the articles use a case study method. Do you publish articles that report the results of case studies?" Such queries indicate to me that the author has already done some of the preliminary investigation of the journal and has a genuine interest in publishing his or her work there; the author just wants to be certain that the manuscript meets the journal's style requirements or is appropriate in terms of methodological focus.
Renzetti (2011, p. 92)

In general it is a good idea to have a short list of 3–5 journals in mind for a prospective article. Some people put them in order of reputation or impact factor, knowing that the odds of having the article published in the first or even the second journal is unlikely.

Others put them in order of most likely to publish. Start with the one at the top of the list. If the article is rejected there, go to the second, and so on. Look at sample issues or articles, tables of contents, and types of articles a journal publishes. Is your article like the other articles? Does it use the same research methodology? Is it on the same general subject? Is it well regarded in your field or your specific area of study? These are some of the questions to ask when deciding what journals to approach.

This point brings up an interesting dichotomy in personal writing style. Some people prefer to stick with one topic from start to finish, others prefer to work on more than one project at a time, going from one to another to avoid boredom or as a change of pace when one becomes frustrating or gets stuck somewhere. Perhaps one can be worked on at a time and place where interruptions are likely while another requires greater concentration. It is simply a matter of personal style, but knowing this about yourself will help schedule workflow. A writer who prefers to work on more than one thing at a time should have that second project, often a smaller, shorter piece, or something just in the beginning stages, ready to go. Some people have writing rituals, breaking every hour to walk around or stretch, or using a favorite pen or ink color and writing an initial draft in long hand. I read drafts aloud while pacing around my house, in a loop around the dining table into the living room and around an ottoman and then back again. Some people prefer to have certain snacks on hand. Find out whatever it is that helps you focus and do that.

Articles, like term papers, start with an introduction and end with a conclusion. In an empirical piece, and in many other articles as well, the introduction is followed by a literature review. This is a summary of what others have written on the topic. It sets up how your study or article fits into the larger picture. This is followed by the methodology—a description of how the research will be done, what the control factors are, what the other variables are, what is being measured. This is so another researcher can replicate the research if they wish, and also to demonstrate that it is being done in a scientifically acceptable fashion. All of this can be done far in advance of the actual research. This is the sort of thing that can be fleshed out and put in a folder for later, even if it is only in barebones form. A draft of these sections can be updated or revised and sometimes that is easier than starting from scratch.

After the methodology comes the results. This is what happened when you did the research. Following that is the discussion, where the author talks about the results, what was expected and what was unexpected, what went wrong, what can be done in the future to further investigate the issue, how the results fit into the current literature (referring back to the literature review section). Then comes the conclusion.

A more literary, humanities-based piece will start similarly, introducing the topic, placing it in the context of contemporary research, then setting out the theme, outlining specific points of the argument, and ending the essay with a conclusion that pulls it all together. Longer review articles or bibliographic essays will do the same, comparing a number of books or articles on a similar topic, how they are alike, how they are different, whether they were published at the same time or over a period of years, with a conclusion.

Once a manuscript is complete it is formally submitted to the first journal on your list of prospects. Make sure the footnotes are formatted as that particular journal's required citation style. Using citation management software it is easy to change the bibliography from one style to another as needed for each journal. Many journals use an online submission system. To the uninitiated these are another hurdle to get over on the way to publication. Some journals just ask that manuscripts be sent as an email attachment. Carefully read submission guidelines to see if names should appear on the manuscript. Blind peer review requires that the manuscript itself not have any identifiable information on it that would indicate who the author(s) are.

When working on an article with two or more authors there should be some agreement on who will work on what sections. One person might write up the literature review and the other the methodology. Or one person might draft the entire article and the others review and edit. Usually only one person prepares charts and graphs. The actual submission process is usually handled by one person. These tasks should be divided up with some equity. In tenure documents with several co-authored articles, there should be some indication of who did what in each article, or an overall statement of how the researching and writing duties were apportioned.

Once the article is submitted it is simply a waiting game. If the article is accepted or accepted with revisions by the first journal, rejoice! Make the requested revisions, or as many as are feasible, and send it back to the editor within the time frame requested; if no time frame is provided do so in a timely fashion. If the article is rejected move on to the second journal on your list. If it is rejected by two or more journals it might be time to rethink how the article is arranged or worded or the conclusions reached. Sometimes it is a good idea to let the article sit for a bit and then review it with fresh eyes later. Unfortunately, there are articles that simply never get published in any form. That is a learning experience. Keep in mind that reviewer's comments are never meant personally. At times it is hard to remember that there is a hopeful author on the other end of the reviewing process and that care needs to be taken in preparation of comments. A good editor will take all the comments and sort them out so conflicting suggestions are not made, but not all editors are able to do this.

It is possible to include unpublished material in a review or tenure packet. Once an article has left your hands and has been sent to a journal its official status is "under review." Once it has been accepted, but before it is officially published (or posted online as a preprint) it is "in press" or "accepted for publication." A tenure or promotion packet should never consist solely of unpublished items, but a full packet might note ongoing research or materials that are out for review or in press; it shows a continuing commitment to scholarship.

Once something is accepted you can legitimately let people know, whether on social media or just sending a note around to friends or your department head or director. Journals will usually ask you to sign a copyright agreement, read it closely to see if you can include a copy in your institutional repository. The journal might allow you to do so, but the word processed copy you sent in (or a pdf version of that) and not the officially published copy. Again, words are important so read carefully and see what you are allowed to do.

If the article is published, or if anything is published in another format—book chapter, etc. make sure to collect all the publication information and create a bibliography of your work. Now the fun part begins. From time to time, certainly before any reappointment, tenure, or promotion documents are prepared, check citation indexes (Web of Science, SCOPUS, Google Scholar, and other similar sources) to see if anyone is citing your work. Create a bibliography of this as well since it shows the impact of your work. It is also a good idea to do an "ego search" of the Internet (searching for your own name) now and then to catch other references to your work. Perhaps a student mentions reading one of your publications for a class or a course syllabus is online listing it as a recommended or required reading. Presentations might be referenced. Either might show up in someone's conference presentation bibliography. If people tweet or otherwise link to any of your publications, note that as well. This also shows impact. If you are cited by researchers in other countries or have the opportunity to present a paper in another country you are now officially "internationally known." This is most easily done if you have published under one name. Choose Tim or Timothy. Decide whether or not to use a middle initial. If your name changes, make sure to note that some items in your packet were published under an earlier name.

At some point in your professional career an enthusiastic young or new librarian might bound up at a conference somewhere and tell you they have read one of your works, either on their own or as part of a class assignment. It took me quite a while to find the right thing to say in return. Here is my experience; take from it what you will.

"I just saw your name tag and wanted to tell you I read your article in library school!" The first time this happened I did the worst thing possible and said "Which one?" This puts the other person in the unhappy position of trying to remember. Chances are my name jogged a bit of memory, but they cannot recall the details and they are left struggling for a response. The second time I answered "I hope you liked it." This requires the other person to provide a compliment. Saying you hope they found it useful is a slightly better response, but it also requires the other person to compliment you. After all, they can hardly tell you they remembered your name because it was the dullest reading they had in grad school. Perhaps the best response is to say "Wow! I'm impressed with your memory. Where did you go to school?" This compliments the person and gives them the opportunity to tell you about themselves.

You may also meet people who are interested in publishing and want to know how to get started. Be gentle with them and provide all the encouragement you can. You are not obligated to collaborate with them or try to find publishing outlets for them (though you can if you wish), but kindness is always a good place to begin an interaction.

5.4 Editing

Just as going from being a graduate student to being a new professional requires a mental shift, so does going from writing to editing. One day you are thinking "Why are these reviewers saying such awful things about my writing?" and "Why do I have to use their oddball citation style?" and "Why won't that mean editor answer my emails?" and the next (or even later the same day) "Why do these writers send me such poorly written articles?" and "Why doesn't anyone use spellcheck?" and "Why aren't their bibliographies formatted correctly?" Editors struggle to elicit good submissions, sort the ones they receive, and give authors feedback in a timely fashion. It is not always easy.

Editorial work can be considered scholarship or service depending on where and how it is done and what institution is evaluating it. Looking carefully at the documentation for your individual institution will give you some idea of how what you want to do will be considered. Editing a book is often scholarship. Editing an association newsletter is often service. Editing a journal can go either way. Acting as a peer reviewer is often service.

To summarize, there are many types of scholarship and many ways to contribute to your profession through the creation of new knowledge. For some people it is a chore, a necessary evil, and for others is a valued past time, and this can vary over the course of a career. Ink does seem to smell sweeter when it is spelling out your name. Starting early and having an organized research strategy will allow you to take a little down time when the process becomes wearying, so long as you are meeting the requirements for your particular job. It is possible to put together a nice grouping of publications and presentations within the time allotted before tenure, but it does require some planning and good time management skills. Scholarship can be intimidating for the uninitiated, but there is no magic in being successful at it. Start small and work your way up, or jump in with both feet, but try.

Service

6

Service is the third leg of the stool in the tenure process. It means different things at different institutions; consulting the contract or tenure requirements at your individual institution will give you some idea of what is expected of you.

In general, service refers to participating in shared governance or institutional or professional activities beyond the day-to-day scope of your job. It means being active in local committees and professional associations. Aisenberg and Harrington, writing in *Women of Academe* state that "The point is to counteract the given condition of outsiderness, to establish a network of possibly helpful acquaintances, to make your skills known, and also to put yourself in the way of useful information" (Aisenberg & Harrington, 1988, p. 148). Mach's chapter on service in Gregory's *The Successful Academic Librarian* includes a two-page checklist librarians can use to decide whether or not to take on any individual aspect of service.

Service can be done at a variety of levels and, like publication there is often a fruit salad aspect, certain things need to be included, but adding a few others provides a little color and variety so the whole picture looks better. A candidate with a well-rounded packet looks better overall. Librarians who have long-range career goals can use service work to position themselves in places that will further those goals, or to select committee work that will provide career assets or the opportunity to learn skills needed to achieve those goals. Someone who wants to move into an administrative position will look for committee work that relates to administration or involves administrative duties. A librarian whose main job does not involve managerial responsibilities will look for opportunities to serve on tenure committees, to evaluate librarians, and committees that set staff and student worker policies. Also look to the people around you in meetings for opportunities to learn from them. Peterson writes of learning a great deal about management from a cataloging technician who was a retired navy ship captain (Peterson, 2005, p. 86).

Committee work and service in general can easily become a black hole of time and energy. Furstenberg suggests that assistant professors spend no more than 1 day a week total on service work (Furstenberg, 2013, p. 121), though that seems a bit excessive to me. Lang suggests only one service obligation in your first semester (Lang, 2005, p. 66). Both of them are classroom faculty so their very divergent views are not necessarily reflective of librarianship. For new hires, the library will probably suggest library or campus committees that might fit your experience and job responsibilities; these are a good place to start, at least until you have the experience to learn for yourself what groups you might want to be on or be involved with. Even if only a little time is spent, it needs to serve some purpose. Make sure that you keep some notes on what you did on each committee or the form of service. If reports or policies or some other physical item is the result of committee work, make sure to keep a copy of it, or at least the title page (especially if your name is on it among the authors). A long list of committees may look impressive, but if there are no accomplishments or outcomes available it could appear that you simply like to attend meetings, with no recognizable return on that investment. At the very least you should be able to provide a few sentences or a paragraph describing what work you did on each committee or aspect of service, and how it benefitted you, the library, or the university.

A corollary to that is to find out how the work of the committee is passed along to the relevant parties. One example is a campus library committee set up to make recommendations on proposed renovations to the library. When asked how those recommendations would get to the architect or decision makers, no one in the committee knew. A committee formed to review tenure guidelines for librarians should have some way of transmitting their comments to a person or group that can evaluate and/or implement them. There may be times when the value of sitting in a room with a set group of people is sufficient so that the actual committee outcome is irrelevant, but those situations are few and far between.

Every committee should have a purpose or a charge—either something specific they are supposed to do or a general set of parameters to their work. In effect, this is the committee's job description. This may be followed closely or there may be a cultural norm that it is ignored and the committee does something else. The committee's primary task is to complete the charge; that is all you have any control over, and even that sometimes is tenuous. A committee charged with creating a tutorial for a group of databases spends months doing so, with frequent tests or evaluation by students and faculty. You worked hard on this, finding a student organization that would be guinea pigs in return for free pizza, and you went through human test subject certification to do so. The group spent hours deciding on the script, months doing testing and revising. The big day comes when it is launched. Huzzah! Two months later, the statewide consortium from which you get the databases decides to go with a different vendor. Another example would be serving on a search committee. You religiously read all the incoming resumes, volunteer to talk with references, take the candidate to lunch on interview days, and then the top candidate turns you down, the second candidate withdraws to go back to grad school, and the third candidate wants more money than the university can pay. The search is unsuccessful and must start again. Or perhaps you are an implementation committee for a new staff evaluation process and you devote a lot of time to planning out what you think is the best, fastest, fairest way to do so, only to have library administration say they do not really want to go in that direction. Or perhaps you are successful and create a new process, only to have another committee decide to re-do in a year or so. Or you worked out a great policy and the administration thanked you and then shelved it, never implementing it. All of these situations are truly disheartening. The thing to remember, though, is that the committee met its charge; it did what it was asked to do. This happens in all lines of work and when it does it leaves the committee feeling dispirited. Just remember, you did as you were asked. You earned your pay. It is not your fault and you should not take it personally.

Committees often also have specific time frames for doing particular projects, but the deadlines are elastic in most cases. One frustrating aspect of shared governance is that it can take a long time to consult with all the parties involved or affected. The meetings are long and tedious. Would not it be easier if someone just made a decision? Yes, but then people would grumble about not being involved or not having their opinions asked. Mosley recommends that new librarians be patient with the committee process, as it can be especially frustrating for them, unless they are used to it (Mosley, 2006, p. 119).

There are some unavoidable service obligations, committees that involve long meetings that tend to veer off into topics or concerns that are not relevant to you. Napping in meetings, however appealing it may be from time to time, is frowned upon. However, there are tried and true ways of making productive use of time when in a never ending meeting. All involve the appearance of paying close attention. Bringing a notepad, looking thoughtful and proceeding to draft a memo, jotting down ideas for a new article or possible revisions to an existing one, or roughing out a new library guide is one way. The advent of laptops and tablet computers has made this easier. Typing away it looks like you are taking notes and no one really knows what you are doing, provided you have chosen your seat strategically. Ask one or two relevant questions to give the appearance that you are paying attention and make sure your typing or writing stops when there is a lull in the conversation.

There are two types of committee work that should be avoided. One is a committee that puts an untenured person in the position of evaluating tenured faculty. No good can come of this. The other is aimed at people who belong to groups whose demographics are underrepresented at that particular institution. This might be a woman in a department that is primarily male or someone who is one of a few (or the only) person of that ethnic group in the organization. There is a tendency to expect that person to represent that group or gender on a number of committees. Hopefully the director or department chair will make sure that this person is not placed on so many committees that their daily work and scholarship suffer. If you feel that you are being asked to serve on too many committees sit down with your director or chair and ask him or her to help you prioritize those requests. If they are internal committees, ask which ones you should serve on. If they are external, see if someone else can represent the library on that particular committee. The opportunity to serve on committees that further your own interests and research should not be sacrificed in the name of your institution's supposed diversity. One or two people should not be asked to carry the weight of an entire population nor should they be expected to represent all that group's interests. No group is that homogeneous and you have not been elected that group's representative. If the university is that devoted to diversity it needs to hire more people from that group. If they are insistent, bargain for it. Multiple committee assignments for a reduced workload elsewhere, just do not bargain away job duties that would lead to better campus support letters.

Hopefully a more senior colleague, within your library, at your institution, or in the profession at large will help you form or enlarge your professional networks. This can take the form of introducing you around at events or conferences, putting in a good word for you with committee chairs, or making phone calls on your behalf. Reaching out to people who might be able to help you, however, uncomfortable you might be with it at first, is a great way to get your name out there and hopefully move into the types of service work that will help you realize your personal and professional goals.

One aspect of faculty life that is highly valued, but difficult to put into a category is grant writing. I am placing it in service instead of scholarship for two reasons. One is that library-related grants are seldom to support research projects, but more often to do specific tasks. In this way it could be considered part of librarianship, but since it is not something most librarians do it is not, for the great majority, a daily function. It also usually does not support that person's job, but is of greater value to a department or library or institution as a whole. The second reason is that managing a grant is not necessarily a research function, but more an administrative duty, falling in line more with service than scholarship. This will vary, of course, depending on the institution and the type of grant received. Generally speaking, institutions are very happy about anyone bringing in money. There are, of course, caveats. There may be protocols on how grants are submitted, who has precedence if more than one person or group at an institution wants to apply to the same funder, how the money is managed, and who does the paperwork. Any grant involving people, including focus groups and survey, may require the people doing the grant work to have human subjects training and certification. If no one in your library has it you might volunteer to go through the training, and this could guarantee that you would be involved in any relevant library grants, which would look very good in a tenure packet.

Digital projects, as mentioned in the chapter on librarianship, can go into either category depending on the project and the institution. Follow past practice if there is one. If you are a trailblazer in this respect consult with colleagues as to whether or not they think it should be classified as librarianship or scholarship. Some criteria might be the originality of the work and how it is most likely to be used. Merely transcribing something into digital form, unless it requires some kind of translation, would probably not be scholarship, but creating something entirely new might be.

6.1   Service to the library

It is almost impossible to work in a library or academic unit and not serve on a committee or two (or three or four). These may be standing committees, ad hoc committees, working groups, short-term tiger teams to start a project or fix a problem. They are a necessary evil. Some are relatively simple. If a library has one or more in-house celebrations or events (e.g., staff holiday party, end of year "state of the library" staff lunch) there will frequently be one person or a small committee who plan the event. There may be a formal staff association. If there are building upgrades or additions there may be an in-house committee to make recommendations or decisions on furniture, color schemes, etc. These are important functions in a workplace. There will be search committees to fill open positions, which often include reviewing or writing job descriptions. Anyone contemplating a job change in the near future should try to be on as many search committees as possible, to see what kind of resumes people are using and what skills people on the market have or are highlighting. Checking references is another form of networking. If you enjoy talking with a reference, ask if you can follow them on business-related social media.

Others committees are far more complex, such as catalog interface or web design (when on these committees keep in mind that it is impossible to make everyone happy). There are policies to be written or reviewed. Committees like this are a great way for the untenured or those seeking promotion to make sure that their promotion materials align with stated library visions or strategic missions. One librarian, whose strategic thinking I greatly admired, served on the committee to revise her library's mission statement. She intended to go up for promotion the next year so she volunteered to write the first draft and used wording that suited the library and university very well, but also dovetailed very nicely with her professional skills and history. It was a win/win. What she did was beneficial to her employer, beneficial to her, and saved everyone else on the committee a lot of work. There are committees to select vendors, to explore new technologies and capabilities. In good times committees make recommendations for new databases and purchases, in bad times committees recommend cuts. If you are not at the table when these decisions are made, someone else's priorities will take precedence.

Within a library system the shared governance aspect of committee service is especially important. Since librarians work with the public and follow self-defined work rules we are bound by policy decisions far more than classroom faculty are. If a biology professor does not like a policy the dean has enacted she could simply focus on research, doing what is necessary in the classroom and otherwise wait until that particular dean leaves. In a library, a policy is far more likely to have a direct impact on what we do on a daily basis. We, therefore, have a greater obligation to help create those policies or at least voice any concerns we might have as they are being written. Shared governance also means that we have a say in how we are evaluated. Often library faculty will write guidelines for documentation, or at least have some say in how our work is interpreted.

There are times to step back, as there are not enough hours in the day to be on every committee that might impact your immediate job. Even if you express interest, you would probably not be selected for every committee you would like to be on. If there are opportunities for input, that might be sufficient. And not all battles can be won. It is sometimes a matter of priorities or political reality.

For graduate students with part-time or full-time "starter" jobs stepping up in situations like that can be a way to make contacts and find mentors. As a graduate student in library science I worked at a staff position in the university library. One of my self-appointed duties was planning group lunch outings. I would contact the set restaurant, get a menu, and facilitate ordering in advance so our food would be ready shortly after we got there. It allowed people to get away the library and eat somewhere beside the cafeteria without having to worry about being gone for too long. It was a small thing, but it allowed me to meet and talk with people inside the library that I would not otherwise have been able to and might have helped me get good reference letters when I finished my graduate degree and left. One of the librarians in a management position was kind enough to look over my initial resume and provide some good, honest feedback on improving it. Volunteering for a low-level activity provided me with access to people I would not necessarily have otherwise had.

Likewise there are always a number of work-related groups. At a large library the catalogers may form a cataloging committee. Collection development librarians will have selector meetings. Instruction librarians gather to plan out library-wide initiatives, compare tips, vent, and talk about room scheduling software. People in similar positions come together by choice or edict to ensure there is some uniformity across the campus and that information is disseminated evenly and officially. Participating in one of these basic groups is not likely to count as service, since it would be a part of day-to-day work. However, chairing one of these groups or representing this group at a higher level committee may count. Showing leadership or playing a leadership role is generally a good thing; the only exception would be, say, being the ship captain on the *Titanic* or the *Costa Concordia*. Unless your personal incompetence causes a wreck, being the captain of a ship is better regarded than being a deckhand, though the work of both is important.

There are also cross pollination committees or groups, things that bring together people who do not otherwise see each other. This may be a working group on a specific project or some form of shared governance, being elected to a library faculty position, if such things exist at your institution. There are often other types of groups or committees that one can volunteer for. As a new hire it is a good idea to ask around and find out what committees to aim for and which ones to avoid. Certain committees might be noted as good starting places, where there is productive work and an ability to create connections across library departments. Talk with other relatively new hires and ask their experiences regarding service to the library. What committees or groups did they found useful and which ones had been a problem. This might also tell you who writes good library or campus support letters.

There may be forms of library outreach that require volunteers. One librarian might be responsible for attending student orientation fairs and new faculty presentations and so on, but they might like company or to have to option of not going to an event that conflicted with a family gathering. Be willing to step up and out of your comfort level. This is also a great opportunity to learn skills that would be useful in long-range career plans. A reference librarian who wanted to eventually move into an administrative or managerial position and thought that access services was the best gateway, might look for opportunities to learn more about course reserves or the circulation system. Perhaps she thinks collection development would be the best gateway, then she would volunteer to be the in-house expert on some aspect of the acquisition module of the library's online systems. A cataloger who thought she might eventually move back to her parents' hometown might look for opportunities to cross train in public services to broaden her library experience to provide a more versatile resume and hopefully more job opportunities.

Professional organizations and scholarship offer the opportunity to specialize and create one or more very narrow areas of expertise, but service to the library offers the opportunity to create a wider work experience. Committee work often paves the way for job changes or career shifts. Committee work can also allow a librarian to reinvent herself, to learn new skills. In the post-tenure slump many librarians spend some time in self-reflection, in whether they want to continue doing the same thing until retirement. They may want to shift job duties a few times, going from one specialty to another, volunteering for new projects and slowly building a portfolio of work in the new area.

Just as new librarians benefit from mentoring they can benefit from being mentors. If there is a library school in your area, see if any of the students would want to do an internship or independent study in your library. Internships are sometimes paid and sometimes the student gets course credit for working a certain number of hours. Bringing in free labor is almost always a plus (ask first in case there have been issues in the past). As an alum of a library school you may be tapped by current students who are in your area for either a short or long period of time. You might not be able to help them find a full-time job, but if someone is new to the area a friendly lunch invitation can help ease the loneliness of moving to a new area. I have moved twice as a trailing spouse and in those early days a lunch invitation from another librarian I knew through professional organizations was always a welcome respite from sending out resumes and walking the pavement knocking on doors looking for work. I did not expect them to provide me with a job or job leads, but simple friendship or professional courtesy was wonderful. In return I have tried to ask librarians new to the area to lunch or to visit the library. It is a good way to make contacts and learn what they might have done in previous jobs or interesting school projects.

Job shadow programs are another way to invite library school students into your library. In these programs, a student visits a library to see what a librarian in various job specialties does. Job shadow programs are usually organized by a library school or a professional organization or a collaboration between the two. If there is a library school in your area that does not have a job shadow program consider starting one. You might also volunteer to talk with student groups about librarianship as a career.

6.2 Service to the institution

Service to the institution refers to involvement in the larger unit, in an academic setting this refers to the college or university beyond the library. Projects that involve the library in the larger unit can be counted as service to either the library or the institution. This is one of the best ways to make contacts beyond the library or, for public service librarians, beyond their liaison areas. Since librarians come into contact with faculty and staff throughout the university in the course of their daily work life they are excellent cross-pollinators.

There are a number of ways for librarians to be active on campus, especially if librarians have faculty status. The simplest of these is to simply show up. Whenever there are all-campus faculty meetings, make sure a few librarians are there, either sitting together as a block or with liaison departments or friends across the campus. As Woody Allen said, 80% of life is showing up; it is important to just be there. All organizations, including higher education, have a culture or rhythm of life. At some places people get together after work on Fridays, in others they go to noontime concerts. Some departments have colloquia. Figure out what happens where you work and show up there from time to time. It does not have to be every time, but occasionally put in an appearance, just so people know who you are.

In a shared governance environment there should be a library representative on campus committees. This, again, is not so much for the personal benefit of the librarian (though for tenure purposes that is important), but so that the rest of the campus is reminded that the librarians are there. Most campuses will have committees or working groups that focus on instruction, on the curriculum, on digital projects, on student retention, and other areas that overlap with library interests. If a librarian is not in the room when these groups are making decisions or recommendations it is all too easy for the library to be forgotten, not out of malice, but merely because people tend to focus on what is in front of them. If the only people at the table are from the Humanities and Social Sciences the Sciences may get short shrift. If there are no librarians at the table the library may not be considered or not considered accurately.

There are faculty senates and other governing bodies. For institutions where faculty are unionized the union can provide avenues of service. Any time there is a governing body representing the faculty of the institution there should be a librarian on it, if only to remind everyone else that librarians are faculty. The experience may not be a lot of fun for that librarian, but someone has to take one for the team. On the other hand, this is a great way to get face time with other movers and shakers (or at least others willing to sit in a room for meetings) on campus. Provosts and deans tend to wander in and it is good for them, too, to see librarians in this setting. I have been my library's representative on these committees and it sometimes reminds me of my involvement with school PTAs; it was important for the principal and teachers to see me, as my children's mother, active in school affairs, pitching in, taking minutes, generally being around and interested. Likewise it is important for others on campus to see me, as a representative of the library, occupying faculty space. Aisenberg and Harrington, in *Women of Academe* say of women faculty, "Part of the process of personal self-protection should include efforts for the protection of women's interests generally within the professional sphere" (Aisenberg & Harrington, 1988, p. 149). This is also true of faculty librarians. By ensuring that at least one librarian is involved we protect the interests of all librarians. In the chapter on librarianship, I mentioned a meeting of the Arts & Science Faculty Senate where the librarians almost lost the right of their representative to vote. If there was not a librarian in the room to speak up that revision of the bylaws would have gone through and the library would have lost its voice on that important campus group.

There is a certain camaraderie that develops among people who serve on commit-tees together and that can come in handy when you need to call people for favors to invite them to library events. Even adults can be wary of going to an unfamiliar place, not sure if anyone will sit with them at lunch. So if the library is having a formal (or informal) function and is hoping for a large turnout, calling people you have served on committees with to issue a personal invitation can increase the attendance. Classroom faculty and administrators who are familiar with librarians are more likely to bring up the library and librarians in other groups, so it is important for librarians to be active on campus.

How to get on the committees you want? As mentioned earlier, to be part of the game you have to be on the field, you have to let people find you, let them know you are interested. Make a point of going to campus events, especially those aimed at faculty. If announcements are made about a committee or group being set up, send an email to the chair expressing interest. Or if you run into them on campus ask how the group is going and express interest. A more formal way to express interest is to ask the director or an immediate supervisor to request a spot for you on that group or to simply pass along your interest. As with library committees, a request or expression of interest will not always lead to a spot on that committee. Being judicious with requests and including a few reasons why you would be a good choice are tactics to use. If you cannot get on the committees you want, bend the committees you are on toward what you want to do. Or figure out a way to make what your committee does work for you in some way, either via the connections you make or find a way to relate what that committee does something you want to accomplish or a way you want to represent yourself.

Appearances are often important. Years ago I used to go to lunch with a small group of women across a variety of departments on campus. Once a month or once every few months we would go out, talk a little about work, sharing information, and then talking about our families, telling stories, and generally enjoying ourselves. We just called it our lunch group or The Ladies Who Lunch. One day, one of the women said we needed a better name. So, since all of our jobs involved computing in some way, we became the Women's Technology Group. We still talked a little about work and then showed each other pictures of our children and cats, but we got table reservations quicker and administrators liked hearing that the campus had such an informal organization even if we had no real standing on campus. It sounded impressive. Groups and committees can spring up like that, out of occupational need or simply because someone does not want to eat lunch alone. Of course, there are times when it is better to fly under the radar, depending on circumstances. Informal working groups can quickly form to work on a specific project or plot to see if they can quietly and subtly persuade the university or campus to do one thing or another, identifying key allies and then figuring out how to approach them. If there is not a campus group involved in an activity that you would like to be a part of, look into starting one, informally at first and then perhaps seeking a more formal status.

Service to the institution might also mean representing the institution to outside groups. Scholars might testify on behalf of the organization before one or more government bodies, or offer expert testimony on subjects relating to their research. As union president I have testified before the state senate budget committee (and, of course, I mentioned the library as well). Other librarians testify at state hearings on their expertise, for instance the importance of museum funding. A librarian active in campus affairs might be asked to represent the campus at local government meetings or as a representative of the library on a statewide board or on a statewide consortium committee. Such groups do important work and your place on them reflects well on you. At these times it is vitally important to be prepared, as your actions have an impact beyond simply your own reputation.

6.3 Service to the profession

This category includes the alluring yet sometimes dreaded professional association. For librarians the large national association is the American Library Association (except for specialty organizations, such as the Medical Library Association, the American Association of Law Librarians, the Special Library Association, and others). It is large enough to include something for everyone, and breaks down in smaller and smaller groups until committee meetings are sometimes attended by only a handful of people. There are statewide association, multi-state or regional associations, and sometimes city associations. There are subject-oriented library associations, sometimes as part of national groups, but sometimes an organization of their own.

Where travel budgets are plentiful the opportunity to travel at least twice a year to a professional conference is enticing; there are always chances to sight see, even if it is just walking from the hotel you are staying at to the hotel where a meeting is being held. However, travel budgets are not always plentiful, and sometimes family responsibilities make it difficult if not impossible to travel. I stopped going to conferences for a few years when my children were young. For one thing I was cutting my stays so short that it was hardly worth the effort. For another the family adopted a dog one time while I was away. Virtual conferences and online committee meetings make being involved a little easier for those who cannot afford to travel or do not wish to come home and find a beagle in their kitchen.

Where travel funding is competitive, those who serve on organizational committees or are giving presentations are more likely to be funded. The question of how to get on a committee if you cannot afford to travel is a chicken and egg question, similar to the difficulty of getting a job without experience and not being able to get experience without a job. However, many organizations issue a call for people interested in serving on committees. This is a time to blow your own horn, point out the institutional committees you have served on and what those committees have done, relevant education and work experience, relevant publications, and then work your contact list. Check to see if anyone you know is currently active in the organization or subset of the organization. Let them know you are interested and point out any relevant education, work experience, or previous service. Perhaps send a personal note to the committee chair expressing your interest. In the early stages of a career or when moving from one job to another, you may not be able to pick the exact committees you would like to be on, but you can still express interest in the organization or subset of the organization. If a national or international association will be meeting in your geographic area you can always volunteer for the local arrangements committee; scouting out local restaurants counts as work-related research. Remember to word your communications so that you are pointing out how you will be of use to the group and not the other way around.

Beyond the national or larger library associations there are any number of other groups that may be of interest, some library related some not. Those who cannot travel for either financial or family reasons will need to find out what organizations meet in the general area and see how that organization's subject focus connects with their job or research interests. A business or history librarian might wish to be involved with the Economic and Business History Organization. Regional Modern Language Association or Popular Culture Association conferences are often librarian friendly.

Some libraries expect librarians to serve and be active on a national level, others state or local. It is important to know what the expectations are for you. Ask around and see what other librarians at your level and the level you aspire to have done. State conferences of are often easier to get to, usually a day trip if you only go for a day, or it might be possible to drive each day, depending on how close it is to home. You might have family in the area you can stay with to avoid hotel costs. State library associations also have subdivisions and committees, elected offices, newsletters, and sometimes journals, for all intents and purposes a mirror of the national organizations only on a small geographic scale. Large metropolitan areas might have their own groups and associations. Some national groups have state level affiliates, such as state or regional Association of College and Research Library organizations. Being active in any of these organizations will let you create connections and build a reputation across the state. All of these groups will put on programs in addition to conferences. This is an opportunity to get involved and help plan; contacting prospective speakers broadens your professional network, and simply being active teaches you some event planning skills. Attending the programs will let you learn new skills or about services and systems being used elsewhere. If you feel you are lacking a particular skill see if others around the state are also interested in the same topic; if so try to arrange a training session under the auspices of an organization. That looks nice on a packet: "Noting that several librarians around the state felt the need for training in this particular area I arranged a training session, doing so gave the library one free registration so I was able to attend at no cost." If anyone sends you a note or email on the event, save it for your packet as a sign of your impact, also note how many people attended. Not being able to be active on a national level does not preclude you from being professionally active.

When physically attending a conference remember that this is a real opportunity to meet people who might be potential outside reviewers in a tenure situation, or people who can help you get your next job, or a seat on a committee you might want, or possible research collaborators. It is a time to reinforce existing connections. The least productive use of time at conferences is to meet, talk, or eat with people you already see on a regular basis. In *Power Networking*, Marc Kramer lists ten keys to being a great networker. Three of them are "Make a goal to meet five new people in an hour," "Never sit with colleagues from your own company at an event," and "Never sit with a friend you normally socialize with at an event" (Kramer, 1988, p. 5). For quiet people or introverts meeting new people can be daunting, but at a conference it can be assumed that there are common interests. Look at nametags and ask a question about their institution or ask how they are enjoying the conference or what they thought of a particular presentation you both attended. Another of Kramer's networking suggestions is to follow-up with new acquaintances in a timely manner (Kramer, 1988, p. 5). Once you are back home send a quick email which mentions where you meet and what you talked about. If possible mention something interesting that they said or follow-up on a conversation point with a note about something you read that might be of interest. If you both need to do research perhaps you might suggest the possibility of a collaboration of some sort. Say you would like to keep in touch, and perhaps ask if you can follow them on a business-related social media.

If your institution prefers outside letters from people at specific institutions or types of institutions, watch for people from those school. Make a special effort to speak to them.

In addition to serendipitous encounters, you can contact people you would like to meet and set appointments at conferences where you both will be. It could be a loose commitment to meet up at a reception or a more formal arrangement to meet for coffee or a meal, or at a certain time and place for a quick chat. This is a great way to make a new connection or renew an old one.

Another aspect of conference going is the exhibit hall. Going around and talking to vendors lets you stay current with new innovations or trends. You can stop and talk with publishers about what they plan to produce in the coming year, or see newly published titles. Talk with them about cataloging or the process they use to decide which books to publish. Take the opportunity to learn something new about how the materials you see are created. Talk with companies that create library catalog systems and see how they differ. As you go collect business cards. If you are interested in writing books ask at publishers what types of titles they might be looking for in the coming years. If you have small children pick up colorful posters and donate them to the school library. It is a great way to curry favor with the school, since the librarians will probably share them with the teachers.

Most organizations have newsletters or websites or blogs or some combination of print and online communications. This is another avenue for people who cannot always travel. Editing association publications or columns within a larger newsletter or publication is a great way to meet people in the organization and to reach out to newcomers. This, like other areas of service, can provide inspiration for research projects.

Conferences with speaker presentations and panels sometimes need panel moderators. This was touched on in the chapter on scholarship, but should be mentioned again here. Being a panel moderator is another good way to meet people, especially speakers and conference organizers. More formal conferences may have a regularized means of appointing panel moderators. If a conference is an annual organizational event with specific panels arranged by committees someone on the committee often moderates, but in a more freewheeling environment conferences can be scrambling for moderators. This is something that can be listed on vitas or annual reports, promotion and tenure packets, as part of service to the profession. For people who are new to conferences and have never given a presentation this can be a way to get accustomed to speaking in front of a group. When you register for the conference, or if you know one of the section organizers, just note that if they need moderators you are willing to do so. Moderators introduce the speakers, sometimes also act as timekeeper and introduce the question and answer segment of the panel. At some conferences moderators are called discussants. This means they lead off the discussion of the papers, at the start of the question and answer segment. Speakers are supposed to send the discussant a copy of their paper in advance so the discussant can speak knowledgeably and compare and contrast the talks. In reality, speakers do not always do this so the discussant has to pay close attention to the speakers and do a quick analysis on the fly.

Those who use social media can get extra mileage out of a conference by tweeting or blogging or otherwise posting about it. Announce in advance that you will be doing this and see if the conference has an official hashtag. Copy conference speakers on what you say about them. Remember that posting anything negative about a conference or speaker can come back to haunt you if one of those people is on the search committee of a job you are applying for, or chairs a committee you want on, or, in the long run, is tapped to be an outside reviewer of your tenure packet. Otherwise, posting to social media about a conference or writing up a short note about it for a newsletter

is a good way of getting your name out there in a positive way, showing that you are
interested in the profession and the conference and willing to share your observations.
Keep it professional, people are less interested in what you had for lunch than in what
was said in the panel sessions.

If there are no conferences in your area, consider organizing one, or if you have
a special interest consider organizing a conference on that topic. Speaking at a conference is usually a scholarship activity, but organizing one is often a service activity.
Organizing a conference is a lot of work, but it is also a great way to meet people outside your institution who have similar interests. Consider co-organizing with someone
at your institution or at a nearby college or university; splitting up the work can make it
a lot easier to do. Once you have arrived at a general overview of what you want to do,
investigate funding opportunities on your campus or within your institution as well as
beyond it. Figure out about how many people might attend, work up an initial budget,
and if you think you can get the money you need, issue a call for papers. Arrange the
papers into panels. If your college or university has an events office they may take care
of a lot of the logistics for you—accepting registration fees, working with catering,
making hotel arrangements, and setting up any needed shuttle service. If there is not
such an office your job is much harder as you will need to do these things yourself.
Once all the arrangements are made, the panels set up, equipment and technical matters finalized, you wait for the big day and open the doors. Conferences need not last
several days or involve international speakers. Setting up a local 1-day event can be
rewarding and successful. Just as being on a search committee gives you a different
view of the hiring process than being a job applicant, organizing a conference provides
a different view than attending one.

Service to the profession can be shown in other areas, beyond being active professional organizations. As mentioned in the section on service to the library, one can
serve as the mentor to library school students. One might also sign up as a mentor
through library associations. Once a librarian has tenure he or she might be asked to
be an outside reviewer for librarians at other institutions. Clemons and Goldberg have
written an excellent study on library outside reviewers. This would require a mental
shift, just as going from being a graduate student to being a new faculty member.
Now you are on the other side of equation, evaluating other librarians going up for
tenure. Some associations have certificate or other programs. The Medical Library
Association has an accreditation process, leading to membership in the Academy of
Health Information Professionals.

While in the last chapter we discussed writing articles for peer-reviewed journals as
scholarship, serving as a peer reviewer is service. After publishing several articles you
might be asked to serve as a peer reviewer. This means you receive article manuscripts
(or are allowed access to them online). You can volunteer, pointing out your publication record and any other editorial experience you have. The editor will usually give
you some guidelines on how to evaluate the manuscripts and a deadline for returning
your comments. You were selected because you have demonstrated some form or
expertise or the journal editor heard that you were dependable, or both. Peer review really is a form of volunteer work and because of that sometimes editors have difficulty
finding reviewers. Your name is not made public, nor, usually, it is listed on the journal

masthead. It takes time, as to do a good job you need to read through the manuscript carefully and sometimes replicate some of the research to see if it is trustworthy. Then you have to write up your comments and submit them. There is a certain amount of prestige, but it is up to you to tell people you are a reviewer for that specific journal. You can ask the editor to supply a letter documenting your service to be included in a tenure or promotion packet. Being a peer reviewer can be an interesting way to be a part of the profession. For one thing it does not require travel or spending money. For another, like reading advance copies of books, you see things before anyone else does, and you get to see what the hot topics are. This lets you know if the research ideas you have are similar to what other people are producing, and it allows you to provide good feedback to other librarians on what is being approved. Remember what it is like on the other side of the submission process and be kind and constructive in your comments. Too often reviewers forget that a living breathing person is waiting for their response and a lot can be riding on it.

6.4   Community service

This is the last and least important (at least as far as work is concerned) aspect of service. You might serve on the board of a local nonprofit or give a public presentation at a local library or bookstore. This is where things like being involved in parents' organizations or your community's garden club go. It is always a good idea to have one or two items here, but the absence of them would not usually hurt you and the presence of them would not help you if your promotion packet is deficient in more important areas. If you feel your outside activities would be controversial you do not have to include them.

If possible tie in your community service to various themes of your packet. A medical librarian might volunteer at a local AIDS center library. If you are on the library's pc working group then service as the computer technician for your church or synagogue is a nice touch. If you are on the library's website committee then being the volunteer webmaster for a community group allows you an opportunity to test out new skills there before using them at the library. Community service is a good place to learn grant writing skills. If you can show any way that your work in these organizations was beneficial to the library or institution by all means mention it. Perhaps you were the coach of a child's sports team and one of those kids later became a student at your college. That is something to mention. Perhaps a contact you made though an outside activity led to a sizable book donation. This also is something to mention.

People who are one of the few or only representatives of their ethnic or demographic group at a specific institution may be active in community service organizations or activities that are of great value to them, but feel their colleagues do not understand the significance of this. If possible write an explanation in your narrative providing a description of the group and why it is important, not only to you, but as a part of preserving the heritage of this group or of fostering a sense of community among that group. Even if the larger institution does not understand the intricacies of the group they do understand the importance of diversity, or at least the appearance of diversity. Several discussions of this phenomenon have been published. Damasco and Hodges, Griffin, and Moe and Murphy all discuss this at length.

There may be opportunities to unofficially be the university's voice or eyes on local community groups. For about 3 years I was on the citizens' advisory committee for a local transit agency. One of the items we put forward and had approved by the overall board was the waiver of a $5.00 fee for a transit card for local college students, including the ones at my university. That is not necessarily a lot to show, work-wise, for my time there, but I can point to some benefit for that term of service.

Some forms of community service can be tied into professional themes. A women's studies librarian or someone with that as a subject strength could point to being a Girl Scout leader as an outgrowth of that interest. An access services librarian applying for a reference position can point to volunteer service at a school or public library as a form of reference experience. A librarian thinking of changing careers to teaching might be a literacy volunteer. There reverse is true as well. A librarian who spends a lot of time gardening and is active in a gardening club might write a bibliographic essay on recent gardening books or an article on the history of seed catalogs or survey librarians at seed banks. A librarian who works with pottery and clay as a hobby might be a judge in a student art show. There are sometimes ways of getting work-related credit for nonwork-related hobbies. On a more personal level it allows you indulge in interests solely for the fun or satisfaction of it, and to get at least a little work credit for it.

Some people want to find some form of community service that is completely separate from their job, and keep it purely as a form of relaxation. These kinds of service can still be listed on promotion and tenure packets (or not, as the person prefers).

With the varied opportunities available, there is some form of service suited for everyone. Once again, review the requirements at your institution, talk with co-workers to find out what the normal level of activity is, and select a level and avenue of service that provides you with the experience and professional exposure you need, and provides some enjoyment at the same time.

Building walls towers and bridges   7

In an earlier chapter, I stressed tracking individual assets or activities. Here is where we start to put those together in a variety of ways. I have provided some case studies in the latter part of this chapter as examples. If visuals help you, remember to view your individual assets as building blocks or construction materials of some kind. If a person's home is their castle it should have walls, towers, and bridges. We will be building those.

It is never a good idea to wait until the last minute to start to look at these career structures. Ideally the person in question will take a critical look at what they are building as they go along, changing course if things look lopsided. This was discussed to some degree in the chapter on planning, to do a periodic self-assessment and ask others for input and feedback along the way.

Major life events, such as a job change or family shift (e.g., addition of children or deletion of spouse) necessitate such re-evaluations. So do opportunities for further graduate study or certificate courses. Perhaps a career headed in one direction will suddenly (or gradually) move in a different direction. The development of new technologies can have a dramatic impact on what we do or what we study. This might be by choice or as a means of occupational survival. After all, someone whose career was focused on catalog card design and was unwilling to change would not have fared well once electronic library catalogs were developed. We must change with the times, whether we wish it or not. Sometimes we simply need to re-pot ourselves.

7.1 Walls

A wall is the most basic feature of just about any structure. Even a geodesic dome has walls, arches have walls, houses and space stations have walls. In this visual a wall is a basic level of competence. Hopefully your wall will be high enough to protect you. A wall is an overall solid work history. It will contain items from all three of the main tenure categories—librarianship, scholarship, and service. They may cover a broad range of areas if your job has shifted over a few (or several) years. For all intents and purposes just about everything you have done will go into your wall, though loose pieces that do not fit with others might be left out.

A wall should be constructed of sturdy materials. The pieces need to be strong. You need to have a consistent level of competence, at the very least, and hopefully a few high points. The greater the overall strength the better the wall will be. If you are a public services librarian and your library offers service to your immediate population (say, students, faculty, staff, and possibly the community at large) via several venues (say, in person, via email, and chat) and you have not participated in all or even most of them, people evaluating you who are aware of this may wonder if this was a choice on your part or if all the slots were full. If there are three aspects of public service and you did not participate in all or most of them, explain why. Perhaps you staff an in-person services desk so many hours a week that it equals what most of the other librarians do in total over a variety of service venues. That thought could be worded as "Most of the public service faculty librarians devote ten hours per week to staffing one or more service points. I have elected to fulfill this expectation at the main library reference desk" or something similar.

If you have published how often have those publications been cited? What are the outcomes of your service activities? How does all of it tie together? In an earlier chapter, there was a mention of having an "elevator speech" to describe what it is you do in case you are ever in an elevator with a dean or the university president or, in larger institutions, the director of the library system. Your wall should be in some way reflective of that. If it is not then perhaps it is time to rewrite the elevator speech, after looking at your wall.

You might reconstruct the wall depending on what you are doing. For instance if sending in a conference proposal you would pull together the assets relating to that general subject area, to show your overall knowledge base and experience with the overall topic. For another project you might use some of those same pieces, recast to show expertise in another area. At most smaller colleges or universities librarians wear a number of hats. One might be a reference librarian, bibliographer, and liaison for the sciences and nursing, the head of public services, and the building coordinator. When presenting himself as any one of these his wall would be built in a slightly different fashion.

7.2 Towers

A tower is a tall thin structure that allows one to see a great distance, at least from that particular vantage point. It is higher than the rest of the wall. Some walls have more than one tower. This is a demonstration of strength, a sign of power, and influence. How do you construct a tower? By developing a specialty or some level of expertise. Look through your individual assets and see if there are patterns. What clusters are there? Certainly there will be particular job duties; are these carried over in scholarship and service? How have these been used to better your institution or the profession at large? How does your educational background fit in? Perhaps it does not for one tower, but it might for another. Some people have one very tall tower, others have a number of towers, of varying heights. Towers will shift and change over time. A job applicant will construct a variety of towers to dovetail with the requirements for different jobs.

Often tower construction is dependent on viewpoint—a specific asset can be viewed in a number of ways. For example, I mentioned in an earlier chapter that I wrote an article on the male lead characters in a series of videos featuring a CGI version of Barbie in the retelling of classic fairy tales. I might combine this with a master's thesis on the history of the corporate wife, involvement with the campus women and gender studies committee, and serving on the editorial board of a feminist journal to form a women's studies tower, to present myself as someone with an expertise in women's studies. Alternatively I might combine that same article with an article on word use in newspaper articles on selected events, involvement with the libraries' marketing committee, and studies of library websites and of online profiles to form a media studies tower. Serving on the editorial board might be combined with compiling an edited monograph, serving as a peer reviewer for another journal, and having edited an association newsletter to form an editing tower.

Individual bricks are combined and remixed as needed for any immediate or specific need. Towers are useful in applying for grants, to show an understanding or level of expertise in the subject of the grant. People like to give money to applicants who appear to know what they are doing. Towers are also useful when asking to serve on specific committees, to show that you would have the knowledge and skills to contribute.

7.3 Bridges

Bridges are devices that get us from one place to another. If you picture where you are and where you want to be, a bridge is one of the ways to get there. A librarian who someday wants to be a library director will try to construct a bridge from what she is doing now to the director's office. She will look for opportunities to show leadership. She will look for opportunities to explore various aspects of library work, to have an overview of the entire library ecosystem. She will join administrative organizations and find ways to contribute. Slowly but surely, bit by bit, she will build credentials that will make her a desirable candidate for a directorship. Or, she might change her focus and shift her bridge, mid-stream, to being the director of an information-related nonprofit organization. The first step in designing a bridge is knowing where you want to go.

After a positive tenure decision faculty can, after recovery period, feel somewhat lost. Now what? If there is another level of promotion beyond that it can be a long-term goal. It is sort of like starting the whole process all over again, only without the possibility of losing the job you have. That can be another bridge to build (or mountain to climb if you prefer that metaphor). How do I get from here to there? After attending a workshop on promotion beyond the tenure level, I thought a good pathway would be to seek national office in an influential library association. I set my sights on being the president of ACRL (the Association of College and Research Libraries), the academic wing of the American Library Association. My plan of action was to work my way up to being chair of the state level ACRL chapter, serve as chair of an ACRL section, and then plot a campaign for the national office. Combined with some publications on academic librarian related issues and some level of activity in faculty governance groups on campus or in union matters, I thought I would have the skills necessary to do a good, or at least adequate job, as the head of ACRL. I had looked at the credentials of people who had been elected in the past and, while many had been library directors, not all were, so there was hope for a nonadministrative librarian. Two of my colleagues had run for national office, one successful and one not, and I thought if they could do it I could too. It was an ambitious long-term plan, but involved enough lower level steps that I could start on it and see what happened.

What happened was that I hit a wall. I did work up to being the chair of the state level ACRL chapter and went to chapter meetings at national conferences. What I discovered was that I was not particularly good at being an organization chair. I do not possess the ability to make everyone happy or the ability to smooth over bad feelings when that happens, nor am I comfortable, in that setting, with letting that conflict exist on a long-term basis. Sometimes that just how things are—people disagree and things go on; I can work with that on a day-to-day level in the job setting, generally, but for some reason in professional organizations it bothers me, perhaps because there are not those small kindnesses that can be exchanged in an workplace setting to soften the discord. So I was not happy being in that role. I also discovered that I did not do well in national elections for lower level offices. Over a period of years, I lost three elections for offices like secretary of an ACRL section. Clearly my voter appeal was limited and winning a national election was not in the cards for me.

On a brighter note, I did do very well with association publications. I edited a column in a section newsletter and then later edited a different section newsletter. I served in local union office and felt I did well with that. Generally that involved helping people understand the contract, referring them to union staff when the problems were more involved that I could handle. People would yell and cry, but they were not yelling at me or crying about something I had done, so it was easier for me to handle. So I aimed to build a bridge in a different location. Perhaps I could aim for promotion with a combination of scholarly publishing, editorial work, and service in local governance and union matters.

Bridges are also an effective strategy to keeping one's options open for career change or for long-term retirement planning (transitioning to another line of work or a satisfying volunteer position). People on tenure track who are locked into a geographic area have limited options if they do not receive tenure. What would they do in the face of a negative decision? If there are few library job possibilities it is a good idea to have a second career possibility in mind. What are the other industries in commuting or telecommuting distance? It might be a good idea to keep those in mind when selected research topics or service areas.

7.4   Putting it all together

Now that we have gone over some basics, and looked at the three main aspects of librarianship (or at least academic librarianship) let us talk about how to put it all together.

As mentioned in several places, it is very useful to be able to look at the promotion and tenure packets that other librarians have submitted, especially, recent, successful packets. Look for commonalities, not only in the packets but in the candidates. What did they do? What credentials did that have? If all of the other librarians are active in the American Library Association and you are active in the North American Serials Interest Group, mention in your packet that it is the primary organization for your specialty, perhaps wording it as "Like my colleagues I am active in the primary national association for my specialty. In my case that is the North American Serials Interest

Group (NASIG)." In other words, if everyone else has a hat on their head and you are wearing a lampshade on yours, find a way of convincingly calling it a hat. Suppose all of the other subject bibliographers have a PhD and you have an MFA. Reference the fact that it is the terminal degree in your field. If it is not then simply draw attention to the fact that you, like your counterparts, have a graduate degree in the field relating to your collection area. Suppose you do not. Perhaps you have an MA in English and are the Business Librarian. Here is where you can use your scholarship and service to create a bridge. Perhaps you can focus your scholarship activities on a business-related area, business writing or the language used in annual reports or autobiographies of business executives, or branch out into other business areas with a tangential tie to your degree. Certainly you can devote at least some of your service activities to business-related groups. For someone with a different experience entirely, an archivist with an MA in History instead of an MA in Library and Information Science will need to spell out that his degree is the required degree for that area.

In order to more fully explore some examples of career management, let us expand on two hypothetical examples from the chapter on librarianship:

Cassandra's statement: I cataloged 1300 items past year, 800 were in print, and 500 were in digital form. There were two specific print collections, both donated by alumni. One was a group of 60 children's books in Spanish. As the library does not have a language specialist in that area I drew upon college Latin classes and a Hispanic family heritage to make sure the collection was cataloged correctly. The library's English literature bibliographer and I worked together to create a LibGuide for a multicultural children's literature class which was accessed 50 times during the semester. The other collection was a set of 24 older medical texts. Processing these books required marking them both physically and in the catalog records as historical, so they would not be used for current medical research. The donor for this collection also requested an electronic bookmark with specific wording. This was a pilot project in creating specialized electronic bookplates for donations; I led the working group that reviewed the project and made recommendations. The library has now decided that this type of request can be honored for donations of 10 books or more. The digital items I cataloged were part of the library's new initiative to make the university's theses and dissertations more accessible. This involved working closely with several graduate departments. Doctoral dissertations and master's theses for the past 5 years have been submitted in print and digital form. This project attached the digital form to the existing catalog record and created a file structure to keep the documents on the library's server. I also served on the committee to develop policies and procedures to standardize the process for new dissertations and theses. Along with some others on that committee, I volunteered to talk with graduate student organizations in larger departments to explain the new process and meet individually with students and departmental staff in smaller departments.

Let us think about how Cassandra might have arranged her next few years at the library, assuming this was her second year there and these accomplishment were started in her first year and completed in her second. In this scenario, Cassandra cataloged the 60 children's literature books in Spanish. She wisely collaborated with another librarian to create a LibGuide and tracked how often it was used. This project would make an excellent poster session at a local or statewide library conference and the attractive covers would also make an excellent display in the library or at a campus multicultural event. Cassandra might pursue writing a short article for a cataloging journal on the project (working title: Beyond PZ: the challenges of cataloging children's literature in an academic library). She might plan out a larger research project surveying collections of children's books in academic libraries. Are they concentrated at universities with education or library science programs? Are they used in language classes? What would be the best way to approach such a survey? She might ask more experienced researchers for help and suggestions. Realizing that there is not a Spanish language cataloger at her university she might investigate consortial arrangements. Let us say Cassandra did a research paper on consortial cataloging in graduate school. Having some familiarity with it she wants to see if there are any plans for cataloging to be done on through a consortium that her library belongs to. She might do some further research on consortial cataloging and try to set up appointments with people involved with that if she has the opportunity to attend any relevant conferences. She volunteers to survey the other members of the consortium and perhaps of other similar consortiums to see if they do any consortial cataloging. Her report could easily be turned into a presentation or an article. If someone else had already investigated this, she could narrow her topic to consortial use of language expertise; this also could be turned into a research project.

She might also volunteer to take Spanish classes (using tuition benefits or at the library's expense) to become better versed in the language so that she might transition into being the consortium's Spanish language cataloger. If the consortium has committees, she can volunteer to serve on a cataloging committee. She might also suggest a collaboration with the literature librarian for an article on the use of children's literature in language classes and offer to write the section on how the placement of the books within the collection affects their use, with library circulation data as a resource, and perhaps contacting other libraries to see if they have similar data to use as a comparison.

The older medical textbooks provide another fertile ground for research. Since she has worked on two gift collections she might see if the library has a committee devoted to gift books or if she could serve on a collection development committee. She struggled with the historical nature of the medical texts and had to make several calls to larger libraries and medical school libraries to see how they dealt with materials like this. During this process she discovered that very little had been written on it and decides to put that on her research agenda. The contacts she made when trying to find out what other schools do with these books would be good source of quotes. This also might start as a poster session or conference paper. Perhaps there is a medical library association in the area that would be interested in having her speak at their next meeting, or a historical or archival association. These organizations also might have newsletters or journals interested in a quick news report about her work on the collection and what she found on cataloging older medical texts.

Because of her work with the Spanish books she is asked to serve on several campus committees on diversity. She selects a committee on student retention as her first choice because it would give the library a voice and a presence on a committee focusing on a topic the library could have an impact on. She enjoyed working on the library display and asks if she can do another exhibit the following year or serve on the display committee. The display cases are small and not always used as fully as they might be. After working on displays for a few years Cassandra realizes how much she enjoys it. She strikes up a friendship with the event planner at the university's art museum and asks him for advice on exhibit techniques. She hopes that in time she will build sufficient credentials to be on the jury of a student art competition and perhaps at some point in her career be able to specialize in cataloging art books. This provides a side project relating to her research on consortial cataloging.

In the meantime, she assists bibliographers and liaison librarians with the construction and design of LibGuides, and completes at least one guide for each large collection she catalogs and display that she curates. This provides her with possibilities for letters of support within the library and a reputation as someone who can be a problem solver for that type of technology. Her committee work provides her with campus contacts and her friendship with the museum event planner brings her into contact with fine arts faculty. She already has connections with the literature and Spanish faculty. When Cassandra comes up for review after her first 3 years she has good annual reviews on her work, and good internal support. She has produced two poster sessions, a presentation at a small local conference, has written a newsletter article, and has a journal article out for review. She does not mention that another article was rejected by two journals and she is currently rewriting it based on their comments; she hopes to have improved it and to send it out again soon.

In her fourth and fifth year at the university library, Cassandra again works on gift collections that let her stretch her cataloging abilities and she has been asked to serve on a statewide medical history association due to her research on cataloging the older medical texts. She was able to publish her research on that and plans to suggest some of the librarians she met during that project as outside reviewers when she goes up for tenure. She has continued her Spanish studies and offered to do an in-depth collection analysis of the library's Spanish literature collection, again working with the literature bibliographer. Together, and working with the Spanish department faculty, they came to a consensus on what the parameters of their collection should be. Cassandra took charge of withdrawing the books they no longer wanted to keep, and worked with the campus civic engagement office to find good homes for those books. The thank you letters she received from the retirement homes with large numbers of Spanish speaking residents that received the books will go into her tenure file.

In year four, an art association conference accepted a paper proposal on the ways libraries decide whether or not to put a book in the folio section or in special collections. In her abstract and brief biography she presented her work at the library, displays, and the student art shows, as well as her poster session and local conference presentation on the Spanish children's books as credentials for her artistic background. She joins an art librarian's organization and becomes active in their committee structure. In year five, she answered a call for papers for a special issue of a children's literature journal, citing her work on the Spanish language children's books and her work with the multicultural children's literature class, mentioning that her LibGuide on that project has now been viewed several hundred times. It was not accepted, but she did participate in an online conference on interdepartmental use of LibGuides. She sends in a committee volunteer form to a national cataloger's association citing her work on consortial cataloging and foreign language cataloging. Seeing that one of the librarians she interviewed for her research on this is on the executive board of the association she asks him to put in a good word for her. Whether that influenced the decision or not she does not know, but she was appointed to the committee she wanted.

When Cassandra goes up for tenure she presents herself as a problem solver willing to step in where needed. She cites her standard cataloging duties, as well as the work she has done on gift collections. She enumerates several of these and highlights those which have brought increased attention to the library. Her committee work has led to consortium libraries doing limited cataloging exchanges, which has decreased backlogs. Librarians at these institutions have written letters attesting to her work on this behalf. She also cites her work with LibGuides and the Spanish collection analysis. She mentions her exploratory work on the electronic bookplates and continuing involvement with the digital theses as further signs that she is working to make the library more accessible to donors and users. She has a variety of published works, a few peer-reviewed publications and others in professional literature, on a variety of topics related to her work. Her service activities have tied into her librarianship and scholarship. She has also started to set the foundation of some career shifts into areas she would like to specialize in, should the opportunity arise in the future.

Sam's statement: As a member of the reference department a quarter of my time is used to provide reference assistance, either in person or online. I spoke at least once to 17 classes across all four of my liaison departments, creating web-based library guides for nine of those classes. In addition I had personal meetings, outside of reference hours, with eight students in an upper level research seminar, and five other students in other classes. Across liaison areas I provided personal research assistance to eleven faculty, three were ongoing research projects that required several meetings or extended email discussions. One of the French faculty received a grant to purchase French-Canadian literature and I shepherded the orders through the library's acquisition system. I also used standard reviewing tools to order books for the collection generally. In keeping with the university's new strategic plan and a renewed emphasis on student retention, I worked with the Office of Student Affairs to develop programs and events designed to foster a sense of connection with the campus. One of these was a mystery night event in the library just before finals. I also participated in the library's outreach program to area high schools, which included a Minecraft-themed tour of the library.

This was Sam's first year in the library and he is nervous because his job description, reference librarian, is fairly vague. The job he applied for was listed as history bibliographer, with duties in three smaller departments. However, another librarian was hired over the summer and she has a doctorate in history. Since Sam's history background is only on the undergraduate level the history liaison areas were given to the other hire. Sam has been offered some of the duties of the other position, primarily instruction and outreach and he is concerned about how to build a professional identity when there is less opportunity to work with students and faculty over time to build a professional relationship with them. To make matters worse, a new staff person is a native French speaker so Sam's fledgling position as the library's French expert is cut short. His liaison responsibilities are now political science, sociology, and languages, all of which only offer an undergraduate degree. He also becomes the instruction and outreach coordinator. Sam volunteers to take on liaison duties to the education program, which had been somewhat neglected by the library. The connection between instruction and education allows him to combine some of his service activities. He works with someone in education on the use of videogames in education and expands the Minecraft tour into an online library orientation tool. In doing this he reads several articles on other libraries using videogames in library instruction. He writes a long bibliographic essay on this topic. It is turned down by the first journal he sends it to but he revises it and sends it to a second which accepts it.

Sam volunteers to be on a library association committee on instruction and leads a project to develop guidelines for best practices on the use of videogames in instruction. It is revised the next year, but his version of the best practices is still something he can include in his packet.

He continues to work with liaison students and faculty. His outreach efforts meet with mixed success, some attract students others do not, but he is compiling a substantial list of events and efforts. The campus Office of Student Affairs includes his events in their annual reports, which makes their numbers look better. He teams up with the writing center to offer term paper clinics in the dorms toward the end of each semester. This provides him with a good selection of people to write peer review letters for him. The foreign language department does not ask him for instruction and there is very little budget for books, but he creates a list of reputable online news websites for relevant countries that is sent to students. The political science department also uses this in international studies classes. During congressional election years he creates special LibGuides for election resources. Sam expands his professional activities to the Anthropology and Sociology Section of ACRL.

Sam is most concerned about the scholarship requirements for tenure. He needs to write two more articles and get them published. He researches the history of online games in library instruction, but does not think he can construct the sort of article he wants from that. Instead he decides to look at sociological studies of college freshman, what factors are important in student retention, and how the library might play a role in that. He works slowly, pulling together articles, and looking for themes and places the library might be an important factor. His article meets with success. He considers doing a survey of librarians and their interest in or use of videogames, but does not want to go through the human subjects certification his university would require. Sam revisits his best practices report. He decides to see if there are best practices guidelines for the use of videogames and online gaming in college education generally. He finds a few articles and decides to write an article placing libraries' use of this format within the general education use of them. He has to revise a few times but his article is accepted, though not published before he has to turn in his paperwork. Sam has created a niche for himself as the freshman retention librarian, which carries over into his research and service activities.

When he writes his packet narrative he draws together his solid liaison work and overall librarianship and presents himself as an integral part of campus outreach, a national leader in the use of videogames in library instruction, and a significant scholar in the area of the library's impact on student retention.

Cassandra and Sam understand the importance of creating a narrative that ties all their activities together. They understand the importance of working collaboratively within their institution and the profession, and of their role representing the library to the campus at large. We assume they have put together concise descriptive packets. They have learned some of the basics of personal branding.

Parker writes that "The successful tenure candidate will understand that, in a truly collegial environment, the focus is less on the promotion of self-interest and more on the promotion of the institution" (Parker, 2011, p. 207). That being said, the candidate must know how to present his or her accomplishments in the best possible light.

Rose and Danner go into detail:

> *You are a major player in influencing how your work is viewed. For instance, perhaps your publication record is not up to competitive standards in terms of quantity. It is important, then, to provide information about the high quality of your work, such as the rejection rates of journals in which you publish, the ranking of journals or presses in which your work appears, or citation counts or favorable reviews of your publications. Or perhaps you have published less because you do time-consuming field research instead of laboratory studies. You may want to point out that recent trends in your area indicate that field research is "cutting edge." Always be prepared to educate your colleagues about your contribution.*
>
> *Rose and Danner (2011, p. 42)*

At the beginning of this book, I quoted from Karen G. Schneider's short article on the history of branding in librarianship. She writes that there are five questions to ask when establishing a personal brand: "What would an employer learn if he or she googled me, what kind of a job am I looking for, what's my personal mantra, if I asked my friends to describe me, what would they say? and how can I make myself stand out in a crowded field?" (Schneider, 2012). While I have concentrated more on a professional brand than a personal brand, some of the concepts are found in both, including know what you want, knowing how to explain that goal in a concise fashion, and knowing how to create a professional profile to highlight your skills and accomplishments.

All librarians, and classroom faculty, can plot out a pathway toward whatever goal they have selected. The first step is deciding on what that goal is. In a standard work situation with policies and career paths spelled out, whether that is a reappointment and tenure system or continuing contracts, or some other career ladder, it is simply a matter of following the procedure set out and meeting all the benchmarks along the way.

Careful planning, a focused mind, and good record keeping can make all the difference between a dark and stormy night trying frantically to compile a promotion or tenure document dependent on memory, and the smooth preparation of accumulated documentation pulled together in a carefully worded narrative. It is not something that can be accomplished in a few months following years of neglect. However, someone who sets reasonable goals, works toward them, and tracks their progress, has an excellent chance of success.

References

ACRL Committee and the Status of Academic Librarians. (2012). Standards for faculty status for academic librarians. *College & Research Libraries News*, *73*(3), 160–161.

Aisenberg, N., & Harrington, M. (1988). *Women of academe: Outsiders in the sacred grove*. Amherst: University of Massachusetts Press.

Alabi, J., Huisman, R., Lacy, M., Miller, W., Snajdr, E., Trinoskey, J., et al. (2012). By and for us: The development of a program for peer review of teaching by and for pre-tenure librarians. *Collaborative Librarianship*, *4*(4), 165–174.

Association of College and Research Libraries. (2010). A guideline for the appointment, promotion and tenure of academic librarians. *College & Research Libraries News*, *71*(10), 552–560.

Bassett, R. H. (2005). *Parenting and professing: Balancing family work with an academic career* (1st). Nashville: Vanderbilt University Press.

Bataille, G. M., & Brown, B. E. (2006). *Faculty career paths: Multiple routes to academic success and satisfaction*. Westport, CT: Praeger Publishers.

Biden, J. (2007). *Promises to keep: On life and politics*. New York: Random House.

Bolles, R. N. (2014). *What color is your parachute: A practical manual for job-hunters and career-changers*. Berkeley: Ten Speed Press.

Campbell, K., Ellis, M., & Adebonojo, L. (2012). Developing a writing group for librarians: The benefits of successful collaboration. *Library Management*, *33*, 14–21.

Clemons, A., & Goldberg, T. (2013). External reviews within the context of the library promotion and tenure process. *Library Leadership & Management*, *27*(4), 1–18.

Connell, R. S. (2013). Maternity and paternity policies available to academic librarians. *College and Research Libraries*, *74*(3), 262–271.

Covey, S. R. (1989). *The 7 habits of highly effective people: Powerful lessons in personal change*. New York: Simon & Schuster.

Covey, S. R. (1997). *The 7 habits of highly effective families*. New York: Golden Books.

Damasco, I. T., & Hodges, D. (2012). Tenure and promotion experiences of academic librarians of color. *College & Research Libraries*, *73*(3), 279–301.

Darley, J. M., Zanna, M. P., & Roediger, H. L.,III (Eds.), (2004). *The compleat academic: A career guide* (2nd ed.). Washington, DC: American Psychological Association.

Duke, L. M., & Boyd, J. (2006). Making the move: Adapting to your new position. In C. Tucker & R. Sinha (Eds.), *New librarian, new job* (pp. 31–38). Lanham, MD: Scarecrow Press, Inc.

Furstenberg, F. F. (2013). *Behind the curtain: How to find success and happiness with a PhD*. Chicago: University of Chicago Press.

Garner, J., Davidson, K., & Schwartzkopf, B. (2009). Images of academic librarians: How tenure-track librarians portray themselves in the promotion and tenure process. *Serials Librarian*, *56*(1–4), 203–208.

Goodson, P. (2012). *Becoming an academic writer: 50 exercises for paced, productive, and powerful writing*. Los Angeles: Sage.

Graves, S. J., Xiong, J. A., & Park, J.-H. (2008). Parenthood, professorship, and librarianship: Are they mutually exclusive? *Journal of Academic Librarianship*, *34*(3), 202–210.

Gregory, G. M. (2005). *The successful academic librarian: Winning strategies from library leaders*. Medford, NJ: Information Today, Inc.

Griffin, K. L. (2013). Pursuing promotion and tenure in the academy: A librarian's cautionary tale. *Negro Educational Review*, *62*(1–4), 77–96.

Hagedorn, L. S. (Ed.), (2000). *What contributes to job satisfaction among faculty and staff.* San Francisco: Jossey-Bass Publishers.

Harem, S., Garland, S. B., France, M., & Cortese, A. (1998). Is Bill Neukom too tough for the job? *Business Week*, *3562*, 68–69.

Hecker, P., & Smith, L. (2012). Tenure and promotion: Criteria and procedures used by University of Louisiana system libraries. *Codex (2150–086X)*, *2*(2), 17–45.

Herron, D., & Haglund, L. (2007). Mismatch between the demands for tenure and those of public services is creating a crossroads in academic librarianship. *Evidence Based Library & Information Practice*, *2*(4), 73–76.

Higgins, S. E., & Welsh, T. S. (2009). The tenure process in LIS: A survey of LIS/IS program directors. *Journal of Education for Library & Information Science*, *50*(3), 176–189.

Hill, J. S. (2007). Technical services and tenure: Impediments and strategies. *Cataloging & Classification Quarterly*, *44*(3), 151–178.

Hochschild, A. (1983). *The managed heart: Commercialization of human feeling.* Berkeley: University of California Press.

Huey, B. (2009). *Handbook for academic authors* (5th ed.). New York: Cambridge University Press.

Kramer, M. (1988). *Power networking: Using the contacts you don't even know you have to succeed in the job you want.* Lincolnwood, IL: VGM Career Horizons.

Lagier, Sydney. (October 28, 2013). In search of a new identity. *Wall Street Journal*, pp. R12

Lang, J. M. (2005). *Life on the tenure track: Lessons from the first year.* Baltimore: Johns Hopkins University Press.

Lenning, E., Brightman, S., & Caringella, S. (Eds.), (2011). *A guide to surviving a career in academia: Navigating the rites of passage.* New York: Routledge.

Lodge, D. (1984). *Small world: An academic romance.* New York: Warner Books.

Lucas, C. J., & Murry, J. W. (2007). *New faculty: A practical guide for academic beginners* (2nd ed.). Basingstoke: Palgrave Macmillan.

Mach, M. (2005). Time served is time well spent—Making the most of your service commitments. In G. M. Gregory (Ed.), *The successful academic librarian: Winning strategies from library leaders* (pp. 43–56). Medford, NJ: Information Today, Inc.

Matloff, J. (2011). 20 years later the making of a classic: Boyz N the hood. *Ebony*, *66*(9), 112–117, July.

Miller, B. H., McDonald, E., & Jia, M. (2005). Jumping through the hoops: Serials librarians' reflections on tenure, reappointment, and promotion experiences in academia. *Serials Review*, *31*(1), 39–53.

Moe, A. M., & Murphy, L. M. (2011). Being a new faculty. In E. Lenning, S. Brightman, & S. Caringella (Eds.), *A guide to surviving a career in academia: Navigating the rites of passage* (pp. 57–75). New York: Routledge.

Mosley, P. A. (2006). Administration and management. In C. Tucker & R. Sinha (Eds.), *New librarian, new job* (pp. 116–126). Lanham, MD: Scarecrow Press, Inc.

Nall, C., & Gustavson, A. (2010). Surviving the tenure process: A model for collaborative research. *Endnotes*, *1*(1), I1–I8.

Parker, C. A. (2011). Tenure advice for law librarians and their directors. *Law Library Journal*, *103*(2), 199–217.

Peterson, V. J. (2005). Mentors—How to find them, how to use them. In G. M. Gregory (Ed.), *The successful academic librarian: Winning strategies from library leaders* (pp. 83–92). Medford, NJ: Information Today, Inc.

Reinhart, S. M. (2013). *Giving academic presentations* (2nd ed.). Ann Arbor: University of Michigan Press.

Renzetti, C. M. (2011). A brief guide to academic publishing. In E. Lenning, S. Brightman & S. Caringella (Eds.), *A guide to surviving a career in academia: Navigating the rites of passage* (pp. 90–102). New York: Routledge.

Rosato, D. (2013). The big question: How can I bulletproof my career? *Money, 42*(8), 92–95, Sept.

Rose, S. M., & Danner, M. J. E. (2011). Money matters: The art of negotiation for women faculty. In E. Lenning, S. Brightman, & S. Caringella (Eds.), *A guide to surviving a career in academia: Navigating the rites of passage* (pp. 33–56). New York: Routledge.

Sandberg, S. (2013). *Lean in: Women, work, and the will to lead.* New York: Alfred A. Knopf.

Schneider, K. G. (2012). Personal branding for librarians. *American Libraries, 43*(11/12), 34–37 Nov/Dec.

Shellenbarger, Sue. (December 11, 2013). The problem with busy colleagues: Secondhand stress. *Wall Street Journal,* pp. D1+.

Smith, F. (2006). Tenure and promotion: How university system of Georgia librarians rate what we do. *Georgia Library Quarterly, 43*(1), 11–16.

Spires, T. (2007). The busy librarian: Prioritizing tenure and dealing with stress for academic library professionals. *Illinois Libraries, 86*(4), 101–108.

Stanley, T. J. (2004). *Millionaire women next door: The many journeys of successful American businesswomen.* Kansas City, MO: Andrews McMeel Publishing.

Stephens, J., Sare, L., Kimball, R., Foster, M., & Kitchens, J. (2011). Tenure support mechanisms provided by the faculty research committee at Texas A&M University Libraries: A model for academic libraries. *Library Management, 32*(8), 531–539.

Still, J. M. (2005). How resourceful librarians can keep records to promote their work. *Marketing Library Services, 19*(3), 1–45.

Sword, H. (2012). *Stylish academic writing.* Cambridge: Harvard University Press.

Trower, C. A. (2012). *Success on the tenure track: Five keys to faculty job satisfaction.* Baltimore: Johns Hopkins University Press.

Tucker, C., & Sinha, R. (Eds.), (2006). *New librarian, new job: Practical advice for managing the transition.* Lanham, MD: Scarecrow Press.

vanDuinkerken, W., Coker, C., & Anderson, M. (2010). Perspectives on …: Looking like everyone else: Academic portfolios for librarians. *Journal of Academic Librarianship, 36*(2), 77–96, March.

Wallace, D. F. (2009). *This is water: Some thoughts, delivered on a significant occasion, about living a compassionate life.* New York: Little, Brown and Company.

Weintraub, M., & Litwinka, L. (2013). *The complete social media community manager's guide: Essential tools and tactics for business success.* Indianapolis, IN: John Wiley & Sons.

Wilkinson, Z. (2013). Rock around the (tenure) clock: Research strategies for new academic librarians. *New Library World, 114*(1), 54–66.

Wiskup, M. (2007). *The it factor: Be the one people like, listen to, and remember.* New York: Amacom Publishing.

Wong, O. K. (2013). *An instructor primer for adjunct and new faculty: Foundations for career success.* Lanham: Rowman & Littlefield Education.

Zakas, N. C. (December 31, 2012). Being right doesn't matter. NCZOnline. Retrieved August 30, 2014, from http://www.nczonline.net/blog/2012/12/31/being-right-doesnt-matter/.

Index

Printed in the United States
By Bookmasters